Light in Our Darkness weave[...] bly different people into one compelling account of what happens when good intentions go dangerously awry . . . and Lisa and Kathy reveal how you and I can help others discover light in the midst of their darkness!

David Bereit, CEO of 40 Days for Life

It is rare in our world today that you encounter true transparency. *Light in Our Darkness* explodes with authenticity. This is an amazing, brave story.

Lt. Gen. (Ret.) William G. "Jerry" Boykin
Executive Vice President
Family Research Council

We live in an age where human beings are viewed with varying degrees of value. We celebrate some people, disregard others, and destroy ones we deem worthless. Yet every single human being, regardless of subjective circumstances, possesses unlimited potential and priceless value. *Light in Our Darkness* is a powerful, poignant reminder that each and every one of us is a wonderful, marvelous image bearer, created with purpose and a plan. Read, contemplate, and celebrate life!

Brian Fisher, Co-Founder and President
Human Coalition

Are you haunted by guilt, shame, or remorse? There is hope for you in the pages of this book. Readers will be shown through real life stories that they too can come from darkness into life-giving light.

Ruth Graham

Light in Our Darkness examines a controversial subject, abortion, in a fairly unique way. The book does what politics cannot do by personalizing the subject through the life of the man who originally led the charge for abortion rights, Dr. Bernard Nathanson, and the lives of the authors. It exposes some surprising history about the abortion debate that predates and sets the stage for *Roe v. Wade* while also revealing the dramatic life journey of Dr. Nathanson *after* his initial activism. And, aside from the already heavy subject matter, Lisa is brutally honest about her own life's journey, a personal tale of "fall, grace and redemption" that deserves telling on its own. This is a compelling and thought-provoking read for anyone interested in the abortion debate, regardless of which side of it you may be on.

Tony Guerrero
Jazz Musician
Founder/President
FACT Alliance/Let's Respond

This captivating story is for those who may worry about their place in the world, wonder how to use their past mistakes for good, or struggle with their identity and sense of purpose. It is for anyone who needs hope for the future—which is all of us.

Janet Kelly, Foster Care/Adoption Advocate
and former Virginia Secretary of the Commonwealth

Many themes run through this chronicle; foremost from utter depravity, through forgiveness to victorious redemption. Another is the powerful explanation of Dr. Bernard Nathanson, a man who unleashed a bloody revolution on America and spent his twilight years trying to rein it back in.

Evangelist Alveda C. King
Pastoral Associate, Priests for Life

Unflinching, compelling, and grippingly honest! In their powerful book, *Light in Our Darkness,* Lisa and Kathy weave together the tapestry of three broken people who followed that thin ray of grace out of the darkness and into the light. You will cheer their redemption and courage, and be deeply moved by their commitment to the truth that every life matters.

Randy Singer, author

You'll never think of the word *grace* the same way. This gripping and revealing story will have you on the edge of your seat eager to see what happens yet not wanting the story to end.

Darryl and Tracy Strawberry
Strawberry Ministries

Dr. Bernard Nathanson's personal journey from devastation to destiny is riveting—when told alongside the domino effect stories of these two courageous women, the result is a heart-changing drama that will stay with you long after turning the last page.

Kathleen Wilson, Executive Director
Mary's Shelter, Inc., Fredericksburg, VA

This is a story of how God transforms our sorrow, creating life within us, until we become joyful life-givers for others. Read this book and rejoice, not only for Lisa and Kathy, but for yourself, and have another sip or two of hope if you've lost your way!

Wes Yoder, author of *Bond of Brothers*

Light in Our Darkness

Light in Our Darkness

Deception, Murder, *and* Unexpected Grace

Lisa Kratz Thomas and Kathy Gray

Epilogue by Deacon Keith Fournier

Cappella
Books
Nashville, Tennessee

Cover photo of authors: Tiffany Baird
Cover design: JD Smith Design
Interior design/typesetting: Lisa Parnell, lparnell.com

ISBN: 978-0-9882870-5-1 (Print)
ISBN: 978-0-9882870-6-8 (eBook)

Printed in the United States of America

23 22 21 20 19 18 17 16   1 2 3 4 5

We dedicate this book
to those who are considered life's throwaways
and to those who feel lost and are looking
to find their unique purpose.

For those who reached out to us in our darkest moments
and guided us into the light of our destiny,
we are forever grateful.

Contents

Authors' Note

"You are always someone's favorite unfolding story."

~Ann Patchett

This is a story about three lives that unexpectedly interweave over the span of forty years, one profoundly affecting another. These individuals were gravely misled and came to believe the sinister misconception that some lives are more valuable than others.

Virginia, 2015

As the sun rises on this crisp October morning, light weaves its way through vibrant autumn leaves, and an astounding sense of gratitude washes over us. In this season where the earth readies itself for hibernation, permeating the atmosphere with its organic scent and breathtaking color, we revel in a deep rest we never imagined possible. The seeds sown in this busy season have yielded a harvest beyond our comprehension.

It has been three years since we first heard the name Bernard Nathanson, and our lives have not been the same since. You see, over the course of ten years, Dr. Nathanson shrouded America in the shadows of deception and ushered in a culture of death. When we learned this, it alarmed us to such an extent that this project became inescapable. Through countless hours of research, interviews, and conversations we uncovered his private torment—the ripple effect impacting our own personal devastation. We came to the startling realization that the lies we believed were fashioned much like his. Over time the revelation settled on us that we, in fact, were more like him than different.

Bernard Nathanson, a Jewish doctor, born in the 1920s and raised in academia on the Upper West Side of New York City, became a political activist who enacted policy change that affected every woman in the country. Driven by negative forces of personal rejection, he took countless lives and impacted millions more. But he became so tormented by what he'd unleashed that he spent his twilight years fighting to overturn his own victory.

I, Lisa, was born into a Catholic family in the 1950s and raised in a Maryland suburb of our nation's capital; where later I became a prostitute and drug addict on the streets of Washington, DC. Compelled by a hunger for love and a thirst for freedom, I spiraled into the dark world of drug addiction.

I, Kathy, was born in the 1960s and raised in Colorado in academia in a Protestant ministry home, found myself groping my way through a nervous breakdown. Reeling from the effects of abuse and the murder of my brother, trapped in a cycle of comparison and perfectionism, I eventually plummeted into mental instability.

What could the three of us possibly have in common? Nothing. And everything.

Yet our individual stories of devastation and redemption intersect with the riveting story of Dr. Bernard Nathanson. Bringing his journey into the light was one of his greatest passions. After interviewing those who knew him best and loved him deeply and with their support and blessing, we were compelled to pen his story.

You are about to embark on an epic saga that reveals how the light of truth drastically invaded the darkness, altering the atmosphere around each of us. It's the story of how light chases away darkness, changing lives and redeeming things that have been discarded. It's the story of a chance encounter that unexpectedly led to one of the most remarkable discoveries of our lives.

Stories change lives. Stories save lives. This is a true story—one that reveals pain, failures, redemption, and joy—one so fascinating you will not be able to put it down.

~Lisa Kratz Thomas and Kathy Gray

1

LISA

"I had to find a way out."

"We shall draw from the heart of suffering itself
the means of inspiration and survival."
~WINSTON CHURCHILL

Washington, DC, 1989

After exhaling the smoke from the last hit off my crack pipe, I knew what came next. It was time to hit the streets and make some money. After all, I had been doing it for the past year. You'd think I would have been used to it, but I don't know if you ever "get used to it." At this point I was as much addicted to the lifestyle as to the drug. It assassinates your conscience and thwarts responsibility, eliminating your morals, ethics, and values. I had no job, I paid no bills, I had no schedule. I took no showers, for that matter. I did whatever I wanted, whenever I wanted, staying up all night and sleeping all day. I was thirty-one years old.

Crack addicts are extremely clever, manipulative people. When we meet you, it doesn't take long for us to determine if you are going to be an easy target. If you have a deeper, personal interest in or compassion for humanity, immediately you become my victim. Your care and concern will never change me; but I promise it will devastate you, allowing me to use and abuse your kindness. Always being on the defensive, my mantra was *I will beat you before you get a chance to beat me.* On this summer day, I was determined not to be beaten.

I fluffed up my hair, put on some lipstick, and took my place on the corner of Rhode Island Avenue near 3rd Street. It was 2:00 a.m., and it was "go time." Suddenly, self-recriminating thoughts raced across the surface of my mind. *I'm caught up in a vicious cycle. Oh, how I hate what my life has become, but I hate it more when I'm sober. At least when I'm high the voices of shame and anger aren't quite as loud—the self-loathing not as prominent. How did I get here? When did anything, no matter how depraved, become acceptable to me as long as the end result provided me with a way to get high?* But such thoughts were too deep for me to contemplate for long; their consequences were too far ahead. There was money to be made, work to be done, and a man who waited for me to bring home the cash, so . . . game on.

Washington, DC, is the most influential, commanding city in the world. It has a thriving, diverse culture that represents many different types of people. In this power-driven city your worth is determined by who you know rather than your bank account. Everyone is jockeying for position: legislators, journalists, lobbyists, socialites. You could call it unique. You could also call it bipolar.

Each year, thousands of people descend upon our nation's capital to learn about our government and our history, making their way along the National Mall from the Jefferson and Lincoln Memorials, past the Washington Monument, and up the Smithsonian corridor to the US Capitol. During the day, those noble symbols of American democracy and freedom stand pristine and powerful. Veterans stand in front of precious names inscribed on memorials, families snap selfies with elegant monuments, public servants and foreign diplomats go about the business of government. Neighborhoods like Georgetown, Adams Morgan, and Chinatown provide great entertainment and abundant diversity. It's a culture steeped in the awe-inspiring people and events of American history.

But as the sun sets an entirely different culture emerges. Blocks from the Oval Office and on the same streets diplomats and lawmakers and history-minded tourists traverse by day, men and women alike seek to feed their souls with illicit sex, booze, violence, and things even more perverse. At night open-air drug markets located along commuting corridors and within public housing projects provide customers from the neighboring Virginia and Maryland suburbs or from within the city a steady availability of illegal drugs. This is an entire culture steeped in self-indulgence and illegal activity. This was the DC in which I was going about my "business." This was my life.

> In this power-driven city your worth is determined by who you know rather than your bank account.

One bright spot in my night was that the bars had just closed and most customers were so drunk that my services wouldn't be lengthy. Men pay for sex for different reasons: some out of loneliness, some out of lust, and others just to be free from emotional investment. My reason? It was for love. I wasn't in love with my clients. No, I hated the desperation in their eyes, their bizarre desires, and the way I felt when I was with them. But I endured all these feelings to nurture the love of my life. A love that made me feel alive and full of energy. An enchanting love that literally had me under its spell. A love that swept me off my feet, allowing a momentary escape from my crazy life. Even when this love failed to provide the utopia I had imagined, I found it difficult to turn my back on what I desperately needed in order to survive. Without it my life was empty and the pain unendurable. It had become my confidence and security, my lover and my friend: crack cocaine.

Crack is a crystal form of cocaine that is derived from cocaine powder and smoked from a pipe or inhaled as fumes. Its name describes the crackling sound it makes when heated and inhaled. As the drug's impurities are cooked out, its form changes from powder to crystal, enabling the user to inhale it as smoke. Crack was an immediate "best seller" because of its convenience. Before crack was sold on the street, users had to cook powder cocaine themselves to smoke it, which Markus and I had done. This is called freebasing.

Smoking crack allows cocaine to reach your brain more quickly than snorting it does, providing a more intense and immediate high. But because the high is short lived, lasting only ten to twenty minutes, addiction develops very quickly. Initially you can get high from a $20 rock of cocaine, but the expense escalates rapidly because of the forever-increasing amount needed to support your habit. Eventually you become immune, so that although you might get high, you never reach the heights of that first euphoria. But for me, the only joy I had in life was to escape reality—I was homeless, hopeless, and hurting. Crack cocaine provided the escape I was desperate for, even if it was only for a few minutes.

After making enough money for a couple of rocks of cocaine, a pack of cigarettes, and a little more rent money, I retreated to our by-the-hour hotel room—one of the many establishments in this part of town accommodating "ladies of the night." "Fleabag" would be a step up from this place. It was an old house converted into a hotel with paper thin walls and one bathroom shared by all. Sticky floors, peeling paint, and mice infestation made it apparent that cleanliness wasn't a priority. I walked in, immune to its shortcomings; I had worse things to contemplate. Markus, my longtime lover turned pimp, was there waiting.

Markus. What had happened to the tall, dark, handsome man I met and fell in love with so many years ago? He had been so full of drive then, with a passion for success. That man was gone. Now, with a crazed look in his eyes, fist raised above his body, all 250 pounds of him, he was ready to pounce.

"Where you been, bitch? You ain't nothing but a filthy whore! Nobody's ever gonna want a slut like you! Now where's the rock and the cash?"

As usual, he was first. Snatching the goods from my outstretched hand, he slapped it on the table, loaded the pipe, and lit up. All the while, he was accusing me of having gotten high while I was out on the street working, using some of my profits on drugs for myself. I stood there and took his treatment for a few reasons, but mostly because as the coke melted, my desire for the magical yet murderous stream of white smoke overwhelmed any other thought. At all costs I would take a hit from that crack pipe to escape the reality of my life. Even if it only perpetuated that reality. Didn't matter.

With habitual crack cocaine use, some form of paranoia usually develops, and it can be scary. This varies in intensity; and when combined with alcohol or other drugs or situations, it manifests itself as uncontrollable violence. Many users hear voices, footsteps, sirens, and other noises that weren't real—like I did. Again and again I would stop and sit motionless, listening to any small noise, thinking it was the police or an intruder attempting to make his way in and assault me. This paranoia would last for hours even after the cocaine was gone. Other people have amplified paranoia, believing people are plotting against them to hurt or even murder them. These types of illusions increase the possibility of physical aggression and suspicion.

The first time this extreme paranoia exhibited itself in Markus had been a few years back. This is also when the physical abuse began insidiously making its way into our relationship. We had just copped some crack. Pulling off into an alley, Markus took a hit from the pipe. While he was exhaling, we began to cruise 14th Street NW—known as the red-light district—adjacent to its many massage parlors and strip clubs. As so often happened when he was getting high, he began to accuse me of stealing the crack from him, overlooking the fact that he had just smoked it. Suddenly he reached over and viciously ripped my clothes off, first my yellow t-shirt and then my striped cotton pants. He opened the car door, shoved me out, and took off, leaving me in my underwear—only to return a short while later in tears, apologizing for what he had done. Of course, I forgave him. I loved him, or so I thought. But the abuse grew in intensity: over time I had the wind knocked out of me, got doused in alcohol and chased with a lighter, awakened to a dagger being held to my throat. And then the beatings started: broken nose, damaged ear drum, fractured ribs, bruises, mild concussions.

> I couldn't live with my addiction, yet I thought I couldn't live without it.

When Markus got high he became a vicious and uncontrollable predator. Standing in our hotel room, watching him take his turn at the crack pipe, I knew I had to act quickly.

Finally, it was my turn. The escape for which I had worked was just a moment away. As I began to inhale a long, steady stream of the intoxicating vapor into my lungs, *BAM!*— a sucker punch came at the right side of my head, knocking the pipe out of my hand and landing me on the floor.

Despite all I have endured, never have I been one to just take it. His size and his rage made it difficult, but I always fought back, and boy, did I fight now! But it was no use. Pulling me back by my hair, he slammed my head down onto the floor and delivered one violent kick after another. When it became too much to endure, I reminded him through my screams that if I was too bruised I wouldn't be able to make money. It was a good point—being roughed up was common in the life of a girl like me, but it was one that could put me out of commission for weeks. Sometimes this reminder would stop Markus; other times it would further enrage him, stirring up jealously and bitterness over the fact that in order to bring in money I was having sex with other men.

This time, just when I was about to pass out from the pain, he stopped. I lay there momentarily stunned: no tears, no movement whatsoever. The pain was intense. I hurt all over my body. Blood was all over too, since I'd been hit in the nose. But above all I felt the gnawing need to achieve the numbness that enabled me to live inside the self-created prison of my mind. In that moment, battered and bleeding, all I could think about was the crack pipe.

Later I would convince myself, as I always did, that I was somehow to blame for his violent behavior and that I needed to forgive him. He had a way of making me believe that he couldn't survive without me—nor I without him. This created a recurring succession of events, a pattern that would not be easily broken.

Sexual abuse and rape were part of my everyday life: the exorbitant price of staying high. I couldn't live with my addiction, yet I thought I couldn't live without it. Of course, living was not what I was doing; I just barely existed.

My carefree days of disco, dating, and drinking were long gone. The 1970s-era liberation that had once felt so inspiring now felt like a pillow suffocating me. Living without boundaries had started out feeling like really living—but its detrimental results were killing me. I just didn't know how to get out. My mind was full of conflict and hatred, with regular thoughts of suicide and even homicide. My relationships had been stretched to their limits. For many years I had been stealing from my parents, grandparents, and friends; shoplifting, embezzling, and implementing money- making schemes that alienated anyone who could or would want to help me. I thought if there was a God He surely didn't like me, and I lived under the illusion that nobody else cared anymore. But I managed to justify all that: who needed them, anyway! There was just one thing I needed—and lying on the floor now, I needed it more than ever.

The coke was gone, the fighting had subsided, and we fell asleep. It was the hotel clerk who finally jarred us out of this latest episode of dysfunction. Banging on the door at noon, he demanded we either pay up or get out, or he would call the police. Panic struck me as I realized that it was late morning. We were out of money, with no place to go except the streets. The energy it took to free the room of remaining drug paraphernalia and make myself presentable for daylight was a monumental task—while Markus lay in bed waiting to be physically tossed out. Even though I was living a criminal lifestyle, I still had a healthy fear of the police and incarceration and didn't want to be confronted with either. Many girls turned tricks during the day, but I wasn't one of those girls, especially not in downtown DC.

We were lucky it was a hot summer day, not the middle of winter. At the very last moment before the police showed up, we withdrew from our seedy, stench-filled hotel room to our favorite resting place: Lafayette Square, regular haunt of a gathering of drug-dependent outcasts. Directly across the street from that famous symbol of independence and power was the White House.

Lying in the grassy turf of the Square, we hid our faces under sunglasses, not so much to protect against the glare but against being recognized by business owners we had ripped off, men I had slept with, some of Markus's former insurance clients, even old neighbors. Grandiose thinking, since I don't think any of those people would have wanted to acknowledge us. But we lived in constant fear of getting caught. Life without restrictions sure felt enslaving to me.

As day turned into night, I spiffed up for the evening in the local McDonald's. Actually, there wasn't that much "spiffing" to do, given the fact that my worldly belongings fit into a small gym bag. The same clothes day after day, the same holey shoes, and the occasional bottles of stolen drugstore hairspray and cologne.

This wasn't always my life. Before I was homeless, when I still held a job, I would have nightly binges—partying till the sun came up with no time to go home and change before getting back to work. At that time my cocaine use was not habitual and nothing was going to keep me from impromptu opportunities to get high, not even the need to go home and get ready for work. I never met a problem I couldn't solve! After a night out, I would duck into the Woodward and Lothrop department store on F Street. "Woodies" was the premier store in the downtown shopping district where wealthy women shopped for Halston and Givenchy and powerful men bought high-priced ties and designer suits. Strolling through the women's clothes section, smiling and nodding at the sales staff, I'd pretend to be on a morning shopping excursion. Choose a few hip items, make a quick visit to the dressing room, and emerge in a new, clean outfit for the day. Bypassing the cash register, I would head for the door via the perfume counter to chat with the salesgirl who still considered me a prospective client. Spritz with Chanel or maybe Lauder and walk out a new woman.

But those days were long gone. Spending most nights on the street corner and many daylight hours lying on the ground in the park without soap and water made it nearly impossible to cover up my earthy bouquet. I had lost my glow; I was being swallowed up by my environment. My chameleon-like ability to blend in had changed into sticking out like a sore thumb. Dark roots now invaded my beautiful blonde "Farrah Fawcett" hair, which was rarely clean now anyway and almost always pulled back into a ponytail. I couldn't conceal the dirt under my once perfectly manicured nails. No longer able to pull off the legitimate shopper façade and after many close calls with DC police, I created a self-imposed restraining order on Woodies.

Living on the streets not only proves tough for hygiene, but most times you can't even see your own physical decline. When you run out of money for drugs, you balance your time between conjuring up new schemes and looking for food. Markus and I were under the illusion that nobody really knew we were homeless. So just like normal couples, we would enter a restaurant, sit down, and order a meal. However, we weren't like normal couples—we wore the same dirty clothes day after day and showered sparingly. Even when we were not under the direct influence of drugs, it was evident something was wrong because we argued and fought with one another constantly. The deep-seated resentment we had toward each other and our individual inner turmoil made it impossible for us to carry on a civilized conversation—which made it increasingly more diffi-cult to pull off our charade of running out on the check.

In our earlier days of addiction, when we were short on money we would run out on the check; but we still had jobs, took pride in our appearance, and hadn't yet reached the point of homelessness, so it was easy. But now restaurateurs began to take immediate note of our unkempt appearance and constant bickering with each other, and they knew we were up to no good.

One day while eating lunch at a Connecticut Avenue bistro we had a run-in with the law. We had ordered several alcoholic drinks, appetizers and entrées, dessert and coffee. The manager of the restaurant became suspicious and called the police. Before we even were done eating an officer showed up, sat down, and ordered lunch. We had no alternative but to attempt our getaway. Markus, as usual, was able to get out of the restaurant, but the officer caught me by my arm as I headed toward the door. Fortunately, he allowed me to go to the ladies room; I was able to exit through a small bathroom window, run down the alley, and catch up with Markus at the subway station.

My chameleon-like ability to blend in had changed into sticking out like a sore thumb.

Before the officer made the mistake of allowing me to use the restroom, he asked why I was running out on the check. I explained that we were hungry and homeless. He suggested we visit SOME (So Others Might Eat), an organization where one could receive a meal free of charge with no questions asked. I thought, *Are you kidding me?* Even though the condition of my life was pitiful, never would I stoop low enough to eat from a soup kitchen or food bank. That was for bums and the mentally ill, not someone like me. If it came to that, surely I would have to change. After all, I did have some standards, even if they were low. This made it easier for me to justify my illicit behavior. I was always more willing to accept that there was something wrong with your thinking rather than mine.

I wasn't ready for change yet, but I was so tired of the merry-go-round. One would think being caught up in a profession that takes one of the most precious and valuable attributes of a woman and treats it as a disposable commodity would have sparked a need for change in me. But I pursued it anyway, believing that personal virtue was worth more spent than preserved. Chasing the fantasy that using my sexuality was a tool to getting what I wanted, I didn't realize that every time I gave away my body, I also surrendered pieces of my heart, ripping to shreds the part of me that needed to be honored and respected the most. Not only does it darken the present, but it follows you into your future, because wherever you go, there you are. After a while there is no heart left to be ripped apart, and what becomes of you then?

I was living on the streets of Washington, DC, literally selling myself, body and soul, for a hit of crack cocaine. Going from one desperate moment to the next, unable to face the fact that I had hit such a low. An empty shell is what I had become—hopeless and victimized by my own decisions. I was tired of being used up, beat up, and abused. I had to find a way out.

LISA'S
Epiphany

"Reality is that which, when you stop
believing in it, doesn't go away."
~PHILIP K. DICK

At that low point of my life, I couldn't imagine that I could change at all, let alone for the better. Never in my wildest dreams could I have imagined that several years later I would be operating a transitional program and residential home for women who were reentering society from incarceration. But I did change. And I was given the privilege of working with women who felt as if they had no hope—like I once felt.

The program, New Vision, was conceived while I was volunteering in the women's pod at our local regional jail. It was an innovative, one-of-a-kind, prisoner reentry program in the Commonwealth of Virginia; and it yielded a zero percent recidivism rate. As in zero individuals returning to prison after completing the program in 2009. This program was for women with nowhere to go after their prison release. They risked being tossed right back into the very environment that got them in trouble in the first place. I knew something about that kind of trap. Being involved in this endeavor and letting my story encourage other women not unlike myself was amazingly rewarding.

That undertaking also allowed me to experience things I never could have imagined, like being appointed to a Senate subcommittee that studied prisoner reentry in Virginia, being part of the governor's Restoration of Rights Initiative, and winning an award of achievement from the former First Lady of Virginia. Just as exciting and frankly even more incredible was the opportunity that came my way to host a live weekly radio show. Each week for two years, *This Is Your Life: Courage to Change* was broadcast live on the Zeus Radio Network for Here Women Talk Radio, and I was its host.

How did a former offender, crackhead, and prostitute become the weekly host of an international radio show? More on bridging that incredible gap later. Trust me, you will be amazed—sometimes it still has me shaking my head!

A local businesswoman with whom I was acquainted was the host for another show on the Zeus Radio Network. She invited me as a guest to share my "story." The hour-long interview highlighting my life's story turned into a two-show discussion. Soon after, I received a call from the station owner asking whether I had ever thought about hosting a show on addiction. Although I had done several interviews about addiction recovery both on air and off, I didn't know a thing about hosting a radio show. "Yes, I would love to do a show about addiction," immediately flew from my mouth. As evident in my story already, tenacity is one of my greatest assets but also one of my greatest sources of character defeat. I thought, *Why not do a radio show? Can't be too difficult!* Fortunately for me, the station owner was a great source of information, and the network producer was a top-notch pro. I am a quick leaner and have no problem asking for help, so off we went!

It was a wonderful experience. I absolutely loved being able to talk with people who were passionate about life! Initially my show focused on addiction recovery, but soon I discovered that the prevailing theme in the life of most guests was not only recovery but courage. It takes courage to change the course of your life for the better. Because of this, our venue changed from addiction recovery to stories of hope and how our guests used courage to overcome difficult odds. Boy, could I relate to that!

> It takes courage to change the course of your life for the better.

Our show topics spanned from addiction recovery and prisoner reentry to relationships and courage in entrepreneurship. When something especially inspiring would catch our attention it would become the focus for all broadcasts that month. Guests varied from top-selling authors, professional athletes, and politicians, to former offenders, clergy, and your everyday Joe. I loved being a radio show host to all those interesting people! But I was about to make one connection on the radio that would change my life—again.

It was Dr. Martin Luther King's birthday, and naturally I wanted to celebrate his brave and heroic life. January was going to be a month of broadcasts focused on the value of life—all life. Because of my own experiences, I knew what it felt like to be treated as a worthless outcast. Although Dr. King himself had to overcome hatred and prejudice, he believed in combating racial inequality through nonviolence. He truly valued life, all life. He believed in the principle of love. The fact that he lost his life because he stood for liberty and justice for all is beyond ironic; it is warped and twisted.

What better way to commemorate life than with an advocate for its sanctity? My guest on this special day was Terry Beatley, founder of the Hosea Initiative, an organization dedicated to restoring a life-affirming culture and elevating the dignity of all women.

The goal for this show was to create an "aha" moment by connecting the principles and mission of her organization to those of Dr. Martin Luther King. To match her passion for restoration and dignity to his passion for justice and equality. To remind listeners that all people are valuable. That a person's color, religion, politics, or gender can't disqualify them from their God-given purpose and destiny. That life is an opportunity to love and to belong. That there is no greater hurt in the world than to feel alone. We wanted to show that we are all human beings with feelings, emotions, and needs—even those who might not measure up to our standards or contribute to our lives. These include traumatized veterans and the elderly, drug addicts and inmates, the homeless, the mentally ill, the physically disabled—and those in that most vulnerable population, the unborn.

The show opened with my guest passionately sharing about the value of life and the stages of human development and that semantics affect perception.[1] She began explaining that whether that new life developing in the womb is referred to as a zygote, fetus, or embryo, it does not change the reality that a baby is a baby no matter what she is called. Taking all this in, I began to think how easy it is to call a person who struggles with addiction a crackhead, a loser, or a junky. But how differently we talk about that same person if he is someone we know and love. My guest reminded us, "We are talking about little human beings, not just body parts."

I nodded in silent agreement.

This is controversial territory, to be sure. Many people believe that abortion is just medically terminating a pregnancy. But scientists have proven that life begins at conception.[2] That means every abortion literally stops a beating heart. It therefore ends a life.

Studies show that at eighteen days after conception a baby's eyes and heart are formed. This new organism has its own DNA distinct from the mother and father, meaning that it is not a mere part of either the mother or the father.[3] At twenty-one days—three weeks—the heart starts beating and pumping blood. Most abortions are performed at the eighth week after the last menstrual cycle.[4]

My mind was racing as I listened. Most women don't even know they are pregnant at three weeks, yet the heart is beating and pumping blood and the eyes are open? So what else *is* formed by the eighth week? I was still feverishly trying to process all this information when she dropped the real bomb.

The abortion debate has been going on a long time. But the source of the entire debate was not the National Organization for Women, not the American Medical Association, not Planned Parenthood or any other organization. It all started, in fact, with one man: a doctor named Bernard Nathanson. I had no way of knowing that my guest's interview with a dying man would have such an impact on my life.

The late Dr. Bernard Nathanson was an abortionist and champion of abortion rights. In fact, he could be said to have created those rights. Never heard of him? Neither had I. Yet his legacy is astonishing—all the more so when compared with his notoriety, which today is almost nonexistent. His goal as cofounder of the National Association for the Repeal of Abortion Laws (NARAL) was to remove the socially unacceptable stigma and make abortion available on demand across the nation. This was accomplished through a carefully devised public relations plan that helped make abortion legal in New York and ultimately paved the way for the US Supreme Court decision, *Roe v. Wade*, which legalized abortion throughout this country.

Recalling her one-on-one interview with Dr. Nathanson, my guest began to share and history has noted how he and his cohorts used pro-abortion propaganda as the foundation for this goal.[5] Multiple times later in his career they deliberately navigated a deceptive strategy with dirty tricks and a few effective key marketing tactics.

Statistics about illegal abortions and their complications were fabricated and continually falsified.

In marketing, the party who frames the debate usually wins the debate. Their first tactic was to frame the debate around the concept of choice. In order to remove the stigma or immorality of abortion they had to move the focus of their argument away from killing another person—which they knew was true—and toward promoting a woman's choice.

They carefully crafted the original abortion-rights slogans in the early '70s to promote the concept of choice: "Women must have control over their own bodies." "Safe and legal abortion is every woman's right." "Who decides? You decide!" "Freedom of choice—a basic American right."

Nathanson said he remembered laughing as he and his colleagues made up those slogans: "We were looking for some sexy, catchy slogans to capture public opinion." At the time they read as cynical, but they are still utilized today in the pro-choice arena.

What was so funny? I wondered. *Who is this guy?* Having spent a good majority of my sober life advocating for women only to find out a bunch of men sat around a table and flagrantly laughed about manipulating women into a decision as serious as abortion made my blood boil!

They used the media to endorse the idea that most Americans were in favor of legalizing abortion—when they were not. But because Bernard Nathanson was a doctor specializing in obstetrics and gynecology, his statements carried a lot of authority and the media never followed up to verify his statistics. Abortion was presented as a simple medical procedure on a woman's body, and thus it became "a woman's right to choose" her own medical care.

Statistics about illegal abortions and their complications were fabricated and continually falsified. For example, Dr. Nathanson claimed that there were one million illegal abortions performed every year and that over 10,000 women were dying because of this. But actually there were only 100,000 illegal abortions yearly at that time, and 200–250 women died due to complications. That's 250 women who should not have died, certainly. But it was a far cry from the crisis-level figures Dr. Nathanson reported in order to set the stage for change.

Listening to my guest recount this unsung history, I was reeling. So these guys were willing to outright lie so they could get abortion legalized. Why? So they could fill their pockets and have control over women? To me they were no better than my pimp, the man who had manipulated and used me for the same reasons.

In another outright lie, Nathanson's crew announced to the media that they had taken polls showing that sixty percent of Americans were in favor of abortion, when in fact that number was only one-half of one percent. Before the propaganda, hardly anyone was actually in favor of abortion! But this approach was a self-fulfilling lie: few people want to be in the minority.

Next, they belittled the Catholic Church as having socially backward ideas on sex, claiming their opposition to abortion was not from individual Catholics but from the upper echelon of the Vatican. They claimed that polls proved repeatedly that Catholics are in favor of abortion.

Last, they suppressed and disregarded all scientific evidence that life begins at conception. They claimed it was impossible to determine when life begins, that this question is a theological, moral, or philosophical one, not a scientific one. But evidence does exist. The study of fetology makes it undeniably clear that life begins at conception.[6]

A horrible picture was beginning to emerge with regard to the abortion issue, a picture I had never been shown before. I had never really thought about how we came to accept abortion as a nation, but what I was hearing was the story of its origin—the myth at its inception. Few people have done more to diminish the right to life of unborn children than Dr. Bernard Nathanson—a man who, through lies and propaganda, deceived our country and created a vast subculture based on abortion. Remember, we were "live" on the air, and here I was practically speechless with astonishment. I was listening intently because I couldn't believe what I was hearing. Why had I never heard anything about this before? How could we as women and a country just accept what NARAL was selling as gospel?

My heart started to beat in my chest like a bass drum, and I'm pretty sure steam was coming from my ears. As my guest described the web of deception Nathanson wove, I silently experienced a personal epiphany. The information that was being disclosed was revealing the mechanism by which so many people, myself included, had been intentionally deceived. I realized that we as women and a country had bought every single lie that Dr. Nathanson and his NARAL buddies had peddled. But more importantly, what I also learned was that this same man, who made a career of death and lies, made a radical change. Like I had.

In an astounding turnaround, Bernard Nathanson, creator of the pro-choice platform, became unequivocally pro-life and actively fought to repeal what he had fought so successfully to enact. My guest's closing thoughts were focused on Dr. Nathanson's last words of their interview: "Tell America abortion is murder. I am all about love today. The world needs more love."

Processing this new information, my microphone remained unusually quiet. In itself this was shocking, because I am never short on words. This was the beginning of discovering how deeply so many lives were affected by Dr. Bernard Nathanson, as well as the events and atmosphere of that era. The women's movement and sexual revolution ideology was supposed to produce the fruit of self-fulfillment, equality, and freedom. That sure wasn't the case for me, nor for many others.

My mind was racing. I wondered how many women had bought this lie. How many like me just ate up that rotten fruit of deception and now are suffering the consequences of guilt, shame, and pain? How could this have happened? How could a country like ours be so deceived by such propaganda? How did we fall for this? Deep inside I knew I had to expose the lie that had literally bankrupted my life.

As I signed off the air I sat mesmerized. I needed to make a phone call.

LISA

Hard Times Reveal
True Friends

"If we have no peace, it is because we have forgotten
that we belong to each other."

~Mother Teresa

Have you ever been lied to? And then found out the truth and
were so mad because you were gullible to have believed it?
Although my cohost, Kathy Gray, was rarely absent from our
broadcast, I couldn't believe that this was the show she missed!
Immediately I dialed her number.

Through the years, I have learned that when I experience
this type of sudden insight or have a revelation of this magni-
tude I need to share it with someone because it usually contains
nuggets of wisdom and value that I am unaware of at the time.
But we have to be very cautious with whom we share a vision
or life-changing revelation, don't we? It can't be just anyone,
can it? Because that person can either breathe life into your
vision, providing positive input, or literally suffocate it. It can

turn from a light-giving revelation into a negative manifestation in a heartbeat.

My entire concept of why I made certain choices in my past had just changed. I had just realized that I had been brainwashed. Yes, I had been indoctrinated into believing that critical choices in my life were acceptable and would provide genuine resolution. But now, I suddenly realized that they were nothing more than a convincing sales pitch that was intentionally engineered for deliberate deception. This horrifying deception was by a doctor who had taken an oath to practice medical honesty. I was heart-wrenchingly torn between feeling gullible and terribly manipulated. So you can see why the person I shared this with would have to be someone who would value my revelation and who would be as deeply and equally affected by this travesty as I was.

Kathy Gray is passionate about what she believes in. Not only was she my radio cohost, she is a longtime friend and confidant. Kathy loves me unconditionally. She strengthens me and adds value to my life. She helps to secure my destiny and has been in it with me for the long haul. This wasn't the first time nor would it be the last that she helped usher in the dawn of revelation.

Twenty-two years ago, several years after my life on the streets ended, I was married and moving into an authentic "yuppie" neighborhood in Ashburn, Virginia. Although we may have exceeded the yuppie age requirement, the environment met the prerequisite. Most of the husbands made a six-figure salary, and the women were stay-at-home moms. The perfect family formula: big houses, nice cars, and what I perceived to be good marriages. *Man, I have arrived*, was my initial feeling. *I sure have come up in the world.* The feeling didn't last long.

Thanks to my background and street smarts, I wasn't big on trust and could spot a phony in a second. Before long, the humanity of my newfound neighbors began to reveal itself beneath the veneer. So when my pretty, petite blonde neighbor, the mother of three boys, invited me to a daytime Bible study gathering of women at her house I was skeptical. But I thought I would give her a chance. When I arrived, all the women were sitting around chatting. They seemed to have it all together—each had a few children, and most were much younger than me. After all I'd been through, this was a scene that intimidated me. What had I gotten myself into?

> You can't hold auditions for friendship. . . . It is a process.

Kathy invited me in with a smile and a hug. For the life a me I couldn't understand why she was being so nice. In the women's groups I had previously attended I encountered women who claimed to be Christian but would tear you to shreds if you weren't perfect. Boy, would these women have fun with my imperfections! During our time together I noticed that Kathy was a seasoned veteran of Scripture. She was quoting verses and had great insight into that sacred literature. When our time had come to an end that day and the women had gone back to their homes, I stayed and talked a while. I learned that Kathy was raised in an academic environment where education was highly regarded. No wonder I felt intimidated by her intellect. On the other hand, I did have three years invested in a Twelve Step program in which I was a seasoned vet!

Aside from my recovery meetings, I was completely unfamiliar with the atmosphere being with Kathy produced—one of acceptance and genuine interest. For me, she was one of those people who just puts you at ease. Within a few minutes I was confiding in Kathy and sharing small pieces of my "story."

Not knowing what to expect, she listened. And when I was finished, she looked me in my eyes and said, "You are an amazing woman," and began to shower me with compliments.

My first thought was a suspicious one: *What do you want from me, lady?* She was a college graduate, Bible scholar, and experienced mother. Why was she being so nice to me? It's probably because she really doesn't know me. When she finds out, her kindness will wilt like an orchid in the midday sun. Funny thing, it never has; her kindness is authentic and remains that way today.

Some of my fondest memories from that time are being with Kathy and her three extremely active, chatty, adventurous boys. On one occasion she invited my husband and me for dinner. When we got there her youngest was trying to stand up in a high chair secured with a twin bed sheet, her middle son was jumping from the kitchen chair over the wooden dividing rail into the living room, and her oldest and most vocal son was deep into an explanation of why he had to finish his craft project immediately. All the while Kathy was playing master of ceremonies and cooking dinner. Talk about multitasking! Whew, I thought—I will never be able to handle that! And never, absolutely never will any child of mine stand up in a highchair. Never say never.

You can't hold auditions for friendship. It develops. It is a process. But when people remain friends through the ups and downs in life, it creates a bond that is not easily broken. Neither distance, nor success, nor failure has been able to threaten our friendship. We have gone through breakdowns and breakthroughs; we have shared spiritual insights and struggles. We have laughed hysterically together until we thought we would burst; we have cried together until there were no tears left. There were times I literally thought I was losing my mind, feeling like the entire world was against me. Kathy was there providing comfort and clarity when my character was being assassinated and my heart was broken by people I loved. Although circumstances in life have tried to disqualify us, it hasn't happened. We are both overcomers, and we've stayed in the fight till the final round.

When we get together stuff happens, big stuff. We have been able to accomplish some things together that we could not have done individually. Our radio show was one of those things, along with spiritual seminars, retreats for women, and mentoring those in addiction recovery. Even my husband says she grounds me, that she the yin and I am the yang. She is reliable and safe; she completes my sentences, and I can pick up her slack. I can depend on Kathy. She is deeply loyal. Her intentions are good and are in the right place. She is willing to be vulnerable and tell me the truth no matter what the cost.

Is it any wonder why I immediately felt compelled to share my new findings with her, findings that left me feeling conflicted and confused? How is it that I had never heard the story of Dr. Bernard Nathanson and the role he played in the culture of abortion? Deep inside I knew that the feelings I was wrestling with and the uneasiness in my spirit would be respected. As Mother Teresa said, "If we have no peace, it is because we have forgotten that we belong to each other." Although I was full of insecurity, I didn't doubt for a minute that she would understand that—she would "get it." And she did. I hung up the phone feeling validated and having a deep sense of relief that my longtime advocate was in my corner. That we had just embarked on another adventure. Together I knew we would unveil the mystery of Dr. Bernard Nathanson and discover so much more.

4

BERNARD NATHANSON'S
Beginnings

"A monster was germinating within me . . .
it craved love—and then perverted it."
~Bernard Nathanson

We were born for love. Love is the most basic human need. Without it, like a body completely deprived of a vital nutrient, we grow deformed.

The time in America was the Roaring Twenties. The "War to End All Wars" had finally come to a close, and American ideals were on the verge of being refreshed. A whole world of new and exciting opportunities for men and women alike were developing through literature, politics, technology, and style. The Empire State Building, the Chrysler Building, and the Rockefeller Center were conceived in the heart of New York City. Swanky lifestyles stretched across the city, eventually colliding with impoverished streets.

At the same time Prohibition, intended to be a guiding light in troubled times, resulted in a thriving underworld of "speakeasies" and bootlegging for a population looking to drink and dance their troubles away. Immigrants struggled to embrace the mass-produced optimism of the times. And the decade that gave us Marilyn Monroe, Fidel Castro, and Hugh Hefner also brought us a child who would do arguably more to impact the world than all three of these combined. The child born to Joseph and Harriett Nathanson would never become a household name, but he would impact every household by literally changing the way the nation thought about life.

On the Upper West Side of Manhattan, on July 31, 1926, Bernard Nathanson was born to Joseph and Harriett Nathanson. He was their firstborn, and in this New York Jewish home, he was destined to carry on a legacy. The famous line penned by William Ross Wallace, "The hand that rocks the cradle rules the world,"[1] is typically quoted to affirm a parent's powerful influence for good in a child's life and ultimately in society. The opposite is also true: the lack of love in an oppressive family system can equally unleash negative consequences on society. The latter was tragically true for little Bernie.

Dr. Joseph Nathanson was an accomplished physician and professor trained in the field of gynecology. Rising out of poverty, near-starvation, and abandonment through his father's suicide, Joseph carved out a hard-earned and highly respected position in the medical community. But embittered by his harsh past, this brilliant man ruled his household with the expectation of unquestioned loyalty, obedience, and unwavering admiration. That is, loyalty and admiration directed exclusively toward himself; Harriet Nathanson, on the other hand, was relegated to the role of inferior, subservient housewife. Not that male dominance was an unusual dynamic in 1920s-era marriages, but Joseph enforced it with cruelty.

Over and over, he subjected Bernie and his daughter, Marion, to the tale of how he had been hoodwinked into marrying their mother and that her family had cheated him financially. Harriet was humiliated by these accusations, which happened to be true—her family had swindled him—and made to feel somehow responsible for them. And as to Joseph's opinion of her personally, he made it clear he felt derision rather than love for her. She endured daily slurs about her appearance and lack of intelligence. As Bernie would later describe it, the Joseph Nathanson household was a confusing and cold place where affection was scarce and humiliation ran rampant.

Bullied by their emotionally abusive father, Bernie and Marion were desperate to please him. They were brainwashed into despising their own mother, whose place in the family was unmistakably at the bottom. This wasn't merely felt; it was spoken outright. Joseph treated Harriett with hostile contempt and, in what might now be recognized as "identification with the aggressor," he conditioned his children to do the same. Bernie recalled accusing his mother of being unattractive, uneducated, and beneath him. While Joseph looked on approvingly, both children conformed to the power dynamic rather than become the next target of cruelty.

> The lack of love in an oppressive family system can unleash negative consequences on society.

Harriet absorbed these repeated attacks day in and day out, but everyone has their limits. One evening following an unrelenting verbal attack by Bernie, his mother snapped, grabbed a razor, and chased him around the home screaming that she would slice his throat to keep him from talking. Even though her maternal authority had already been damaged by that point, this threat from his mother, the one with whom a child's first love bond is created, would have been traumatic. Bernie and Marion, through no real choice of their own, had that bond violently broken.

Regardless of her torment, Harriet clung to her faith and was determined to pass it along to her children. She insisted on weekly Shabbat service at Friday night dinners and was granted this latitude. But the service was watered down and brief; the air was thick with silent ridicule from her husband. She would do her best to ignore him, gently kissing Bernie's cheek and then Marion's. Shabbat was the only time affection was openly given to the children.

> *Y'varekh'kha Adonai v'yishmerekha.*
> *Ya'er Adonai panav eleikha vichunekka.*
> *Yissa Adonai panav eleikha v'yasem l'kha shalom.*

> May Adonai bless you and keep you.
> May Adonai make His face shine on you and show you His favor.
> May Adonai lift up His face toward you and give you peace.[2]

But belief in God was something Bernie's father had abandoned years before, having replaced it with the pursuit of the all-powerful intellect. He did decree that Bernie be thoroughly educated in the Jewish tradition—though not for any reason that would please his wife. Three times a week after his immersion in the finest of public education, Bernie would attend Cheder, a Hebrew School, as well as Hebrew Sunday school. There the concept of God was being built up in this bright, perceptive boy, only to be deliberately torn down at home. At home, Bernie was routinely subjected to his father's prodding questions. He was made to recite what he had learned about God and then shamed for what he had shared as it was picked apart and contradicted.

Harriet Nathanson guarded what little she could of her faith and what limited opportunity she had to show affection to her children. Crumbs were what she lived on, and crumbs were all she had to give. But the effect was more confusion. Her Friday night Shabbat, a beautiful tradition representing redemption and the merciful protection of a powerful God, served her children as a warning: any fool who trusts in God will never be respected.

Amid the discordant views in the Nathanson home, Bernie was not encouraged to make space for inner contemplation—or given the luxury of his own opinion. Though he would later describe himself as an impressionable and sensitive boy with a childlike spiritual curiosity about the world and God, any question of the sort would be answered by his father's ridicule. It would be many years before his interest in making a spiritual connection would be recognized, let alone satisfied.

There were many other moral contradictions to be managed in the Nathanson home. His inborn love for his mother conflicted with his father's encouragement of hateful behavior toward her. Joseph absolutely forbade lying, yet repeatedly and cavalierly lied to Harriett about his extramarital affairs. It was not unusual for Bernie's father to arrive home late, after a night with his mistress, only to criticize his wife for not having anticipated when to have a warm supper on the table. Confused, Bernie's emotional damage manifested itself in numerous physical maladies in his young body. He actually thought he was dying from a heart attack at the age of twelve and wrote a will leaving his possessions to his sister. His entire world was a frightening and lonely place. And one clear message he received was that lying was wrong—unless it was done to control a woman.

In Bernie's family system intelligence was idolized, even worshipped. Bernie was in awe of Joseph, the center of his universe, even as his resentment of him grew. He had inherited his father's insatiable thirst for knowledge and would attempt to take on Joseph Nathanson intellectually, hoping to win his approval, but also as an act of defiance. They argued over facts, dates, politics, and finances—rarely anything of moral or philosophical value—and his father always emerged the winner.

Looking back, Bernie recognized that to escape the disappointment of his real life, he developed a fantasy life. In the 1930s, the crackling black and white "talkies" had grown in popularity as an inexpensive pastime, and he clung to them as a precious retreat. An alternate reality at the movie theater served as an escape from a chaotic life. Bernie would sit close to the screen, hidden in the darkness, transported to another world. Swept away by the heroic men and women of the big screen, he succeeded in holding his reality, confusion, and fears at bay.

> Swept away by the heroic men and women of the big screen, he succeeded in holding his reality, confusion, and fears at bay.

Those escapes brought temporary relief—like the cocaine euphoria Lisa would cling to years later. But as no fantasy can mend the real brokenness of a human heart, Bernie's needs, like Lisa's, remained suppressed and neglected. And his childhood needs weren't the only ones unmet in the family.

Bernie was a firsthand witness to the degraded dignity of both females close to him. His little sister Marion, a tomboy of sorts, was energetic, active, and loved sports. Observing the intense and irrational abuse her father hurled at her mother, she became his loyal ally, which alienated her from her mother's love. She parroted Joseph's words, took on his attitudes and beliefs, and even mimicked his walk.

Marion took on the role of puppet with Joseph as the puppet master. Any chance for a real bond between Bernie and his sister shriveled as Marion, little by little, lost her own identity in the all-consuming pursuit of their father's approval. Joseph doted on her and later described her as his "little girl, charming,

vivacious and with beautiful blue eyes."[3] But his iron clutch
on her eventually drained the light from those vibrant eyes.
A dictator in every area, he arranged her marriage to a den-
tist after she graduated from college. Later, when her husband
refused to be controlled by his father-in-law, Joseph demanded
she divorce him, and Marion complied. Leaving her comfortable home, she moved her three children into a ground-floor
apartment near her father, but life did not improve for her.
Marinating in a toxic mix of her father's narcissism and neglect,
at age forty-nine Marion committed suicide with an overdose
of sedatives.

Bernie felt powerless to change the drama unfolding in
the lives of his mother and his sister. He watched as his father
robbed them of their dignity and they forfeited their individ-
uality. As a teenager he had finally taken a courageous stand
against his father, refusing to further degrade his mother, but it
did little to change her life. She faded into a ghost of a woman,
and his sister eventually faded from this world.

The years that led Bernie from infancy to adulthood were
filled with demands, conflict, and confusion. His entire life he
had endured combative, belittling interactions with this man
who dominated every facet of his life. Scorn emptied him of
faith. He was cut off from both paternal and maternal love. His
intellect flourished with a stellar education, but his soul with-
ered in darkness from neglect. He was forced to either choose
to protect his mother or become an ally to his father. He later
said that this drove him to forge his own brand of rebellion—a
twisted path that would lead him to choose intellect over integrity, logic over love.

Not surprisingly, much of his rebellion was secretly directed
toward his father, at whom he could only retaliate in small,
symbolic ways. Joseph Nathanson was obsessed with Abraham
Lincoln: Bernie determined to show absolutely no interest in

Lincoln. Although he became combative with his father intellectually and in family relationships, it failed to effect any real change. Powerless against him in any significant way, Bernie's anger remained unresolved for many years. His decisions, too, were shaped by reacting against what he hated instead of choosing his own pursuits. His natural need for love and compassion was increasingly equated with—or buried by—an obsession for knowledge. As the future Dr. Bernard Nathanson later described, "A monster was germinating within me. The monster recognized nothing but utility; respected nothing but strength of purpose; craved love—and then perverted it."[4]

5

LISA'S
Childhood

"In every conceivable manner, the family is a link to our past,
a bridge to our future."

~ALEX HALEY

In every era with its unique challenges and atmosphere, children wrestle with the meaning of their value and self-worth. Bernie Nathanson wasn't the only one struggling with his identity. In the year 1959—the year of Barbie dolls, *Bonanza*, and *Ben Hur*—I came into the world. It was a simpler time for many, but not for all. People were proud to be Americans; our country was growing economically and socially. New ideas were emerging and taking hold, and media was on the rise. More families had televisions in their homes, and AM radio was the most popular forum for news and music in the country. While most women were busy raising children and making their house into a home, men were the primary breadwinners, with an average yearly income of $2,992.

I was born in a small coal mining town near Wilkes-Barre, Pennsylvania. My parents grew up there and met there. Both of my parents, born in the 1930s, were from hard-working, lower-income families and, like many others, had experienced dysfunction in their upbringing. I call their brand of dysfunction "love starvation"—the kind of love that does not allow you to accept yourself for who you are and just be happy being you.

My father was the baby of a family of six. His father died from coal workers' pneumoconiosis—"black lung"—when he was twelve, so at an early age he began to help support the family through odd jobs and newspaper delivery. He went on to graduate from high school and join the US Marine Corps. After his tour of duty he returned to Pennsylvania, graduated from college, and met my mother.

My mother was an only child and lived in the house with her mother, grandmother, aunt, and uncles. Due to my grandmother's lifestyle, my mother herself underwent severe judgment in the community: being born out of wedlock had a much different stigma in previous decades than it does today, and it was a subject that wasn't discussed in my mother's home. My grandmother was gossiped about as a harlot or "loose" woman. For her daughter, it was a hard pill to swallow. The shame she experienced forced her to question her identity, family, and background.

Although I was shown love as a child, the only way my parents knew to express it was the way they had been shown love—conditionally. They probably didn't even realize that I perceived our relationship to be conditional, and perception molds reality. If I was obedient and met their expectations, whether it was being quiet during a TV show or getting good grades, I felt loved. But when I fell short and made mistakes, doing things a normal young girl would do, I felt their love was withdrawn from me, and I felt ashamed and embarrassed. As anyone who has experienced love based on behavior can attest, it's impossible to feel "good enough." I began to internalize a sense of inadequacy, which magnified any flaws and amplified feelings of shame. Instead of feeling secure and happy, I felt anger and fear. Ultimately this created in me a sense of unworthiness, which drove me to seek external sources of acceptance and security.

In 1964 I was five years old and was big sis to two baby brothers. We lived in a modest brick home in a typical neighborhood in the Maryland suburbs. On my daily walk home from Our Lady of Sorrows grade school, I would pass through a playground and over a bridge. One day, stopping for a moment on the bridge, I gazed into the trickling water and wondered, *If I fell, in would anyone miss me?* My second thought was, *Maybe the world would be better off without me.* I was always aware of a nagging sense of pain. At home I was subjected to hurtful words and physical outbursts. I blamed myself for how my mom treated me. At the time, I didn't realize the negative generational impact that my grandmother had had on my mother and how it was affecting me; but this is how it all begins—in our minds. This is where the battlefield of deception truly lies.

It was career day in Sister Rita Marie's kindergarten class, and all my fellow students began to share about their fathers' occupations. Although my father was an auditor for the government, I didn't really understand what that was, and it didn't seem too glamorous. Without hesitation, I blurted out that he owned a movie theatre and could get the class any movie we wanted to watch. With one sentence, just a few words, I was able to wipe away low self-worth, gaining admiration and attention from my fellow students, which I so desperately desired.

It was a revelation. All I could think about was the elation, the acceptance and freedom I felt when I was admired by my classmates. What started as a tall tale became a modus operandi. As the saying goes, "If you tell the truth, you won't have to worry about keeping track of your lies." I was about to become a living example of it.

I fabricated stories for my benefit, bald-faced lies to cover my unsatisfactory behavior. I omitted information, told white lies, told "emergency" lies. I exaggerated and mislead. The lies gave me short-term gratification. It would be years before I began to realize the damage and havoc they could produce. The paradox was that every lie tore down whatever integrity might have developed within me. Deceit also prevented me from true intimacy, since when you lie you always have to be guarded, never able to share what is really going on inside. The continual façade prevents meaningful communication. Truth itself becomes subjective for the liar. And the more you lie, the more you need to lie, because when you get caught, you lie to get out. It is a never-ending cycle. Lies brought self-assassination and pain not only to me, but also to those who came into contact with me. Once I started down this path it would be years before I realized the refreshing freedom that comes from honesty.

> The paradox was that every lie tore down whatever integrity might have developed within me.

Lying was my first coping mechanism and a constant companion throughout my early life. It enabled me to rationalize my actions, to be selfish and gain a false sense of security in life, and to maintain secrets. Some coping methods, of course, are healthy: deep breathing, exercise, helpful hobbies, meditation, prayer. But there is also destructive behavior, an unconscious process of discovering relief that creates fantasy that only worsens our problems. Convinced that these methods offer an easy way out, we don't realize that using such mechanisms as a form of escape can be lethal.

On another day, when I was walking home from school, there was a group of kids gathering in the road around a large trash can. I was shocked, but curious to see dozens of explicit pornographic pictures discarded there. I wanted to talk to my mom about what I saw, but I instinctively knew this was something she would not want to discuss and that she would get angry at me for asking. The natural curiosity of childhood needs to be dealt with carefully by an adult, with a distinction made between sex and pornography—porn being an unhealthy response to a healthy curiosity. Thinking about those pictures later, I knew she would be mad at me for looking at them and that I would feel ashamed for having asked. I kept those feelings a secret, much like secrets that were kept in my mother's home when she was growing up.

During that same week, while I was playing at a neighbor's house, an older brother of one of my classmates exposed himself to me. Again, I internalized this as somehow being my fault. The images of these two circumstances played in my mind like slides on a projector, burning into my psyche, leaving me feeling disgraced and guilty. I started believing that I was a "bad girl."

Today we know that sexually arousing images (pornography) leave an imprint on the brain and can involuntarily trigger a memory. Pornography causes similar damage to the brain that occurs from substances such as cocaine or methamphetamine.[1] Aside from that damage, porn underscores the single standard of beauty that our society cultivates—a standard that no real woman can live up to. It doesn't really matter how smart you are, just as long as you are physically beautiful. Specifically, 36"-24"-36". Not understanding my motivation, with great determination I began the quest for perfection at the age of five.

Never did I think that that love starvation, a few little lies, low self-worth, or faulty thinking would lead me to years of self-destruction and a suicide attempt. In my early adulthood I would go on to try just about everything to bring excitement and purpose into my life. Besides my substance abuse, there were job changes and what I call geographic cures, attempts to start over without really fixing the problem I left behind. There were bouts of kinky sex, relationships with the rich and famous, and living on the edge. There were no limits, no boundaries. And always the result was nil. I was confused, unable to get answers to my questions. I was living with no clear explanation of what is right or wrong. I hungered for more . . . but more of what, I didn't know.

KATHY'S
Early Years

Define yourself radically as one beloved by God.
This is the true self. Every other identity is illusion.

~BRENNAN MANNING

Upside down again. Feet in the air, my wavy blonde hair brushed along the brown shag carpet as I wobbled hand over hand down the hallway and turned the corner into the living room. Grinning as I lost my balance, I somersaulted out of the handstand and flopped on the floor. Pushing off from my landing spot, I cartwheeled my way into the kitchen where my mom stood browning hamburger meat for supper. A smile spread over her face and my grin broadened as I heard her exclaim, for the umpteenth time, "Kathy, I swear, if the rapture comes anytime soon you'll go up feet first!"

Ten years earlier, two events had marked my grand entrance into this world in 1962. My birth was followed by a frenzied sixty seconds until the doctor resorted to mouth-to-mouth resuscitation forcing me to take my first breath, and astronaut John Glenn and Vice President Lyndon B. Johnson paraded past my hospital window. I joke that holding my breath was my first act of defiance and the parade was staged to celebrate my arrival, with an elaborate cover story, of course. I've come to think those events illustrate two character flaws that caused me no end of trouble: stubbornness, and the belief that everything around me is somehow connected to me—in other words, that I carry some intangible responsibility for circumstances beyond my control.

Swept up in their momentum, the line where they stopped and I began blurred.

In an era dominated by a thrilling space race, the intoxicating Beatles, and the controversial war in Viet Nam, my early years were spent in beautiful Colorado sheltered in a conservative evangelical home. Devoted Christians and eventually full-time ministry workers, my parents were decidedly intentional about living out their faith in practical ways. My older brother and younger sisters and I spent our days in an atmosphere filled with humor, music, extended family, hospitality, and religious training. My mom truly had a knack for making religious education exciting through games and contests and church clubs. Outgoing and leaning toward the competitive side, I absolutely ate it up. Every time the church doors were open, you can be sure we were there—and I didn't mind a bit.

Both of my parents are highly intelligent, self-motivated, and personable. A former professor, my dad stressed the value of academic achievement along with spirituality. My mom, also an academician, invested her heart and soul into our education and training. Our home hosted countless people who joined us for meals and gatherings. Missionaries and other guests stayed with us frequently. Being the oldest girl, I relished trying to be my mom's right hand—setting the table, serving as "kitchen runner" during meals, and helping with my younger sisters. This role gradually became the identity I wholeheartedly adopted.

I felt valuable when I was contributing. I watched as numerous people came to them for mentoring and advice.

Swept up in their momentum, the line where they stopped and I began blurred. Over time, mesmerized by all that was going on around me, I began to allow my identity, my sense of self and purpose, to slip away. I lost myself in the identity of my family. After all, if I focused on someone else, I didn't have to think so much about my own life—and there were some things I didn't want to think about. So I adopted their life as my own. For some of us, losing ourselves in the more exciting life of an admired movie star or athlete is dangerously enticing. Even a friend whose life seems better than ours will do in filling out our identity: I'm so-and-so's friend. That's how it was for me.

But the deeper reality for me as a little girl in my bedroom alone under the covers was that I dreaded going to sleep. Every night. Not just because I didn't want to miss what was happening for those who were awake, but because of what would happen in my sleep. Vivid and terrifying dreams tormented me many nights each week. Occasionally I would have an amazing dream, like the one in which I was flying in the night sky, exhilarated and free. More often though, it was the repeated thrill-turned-nightmare of flying down the basement steps only to land in darkness, unable to turn on a light and helpless to run up the stairs and out of danger. Even more distressing was often being startled awake, sensing an evil presence and seeing figures or snakes in my room.

One evening etched in my memory is when my little sister and I decided to camp out in the living room. In our sleeping bags we snuggled in our flannel nightgowns under the silky material and giggled incessantly until our fatigue overtook us and we drifted off to sleep. What seemed like only minutes later, my eyes flew open as I heard a loud crash and someone yelling. I watched in horror as a dark figure holding a machine gun broke through the window and started spraying gunfire. I scrambled out of my sleeping bag screaming in terror, waking the rest of the family. My parents flew out of bed and rushed to the living room, turning on the light as they came to help. Everything in the room looked normal. Except for me. It had all been a nightmare.

"Not normal" is how I felt much of the time. My mom and dad would do everything they could think of to help me sleep peacefully. They comforted me, prayed for me, and left a nightlight on so I wouldn't be terrified in the dark. They set up a cassette player that quietly played recordings of the psalms or calming music while I slept. But the nightmares continued. This was so confusing to me because I already knew God, who pushes back the darkness with his soothing light flooding his children with order and peace. Why wasn't I experiencing any relief?

To make matters worse, I began having panic attacks in early elementary school whenever I was dropped off for an activity. My ears would fill with a roaring sound, the room would spin, my heart would pound wildly, my skin would prickle, and I was tempted to scream and cry at the same time. I felt like I was about to die. This awful feeling would especially spring out of the shadows when I was dropped off at the downtown YMCA for gymnastics. I remember how even though I was only eight, each time we drove to an activity my eyes were on the street signs memorizing the routes home, routes that would take me more than an hour to walk alone. In the back of my mind I was always thinking, *What if nobody comes back to pick me up? I'll have to walk home by myself.*

Almost worse than the panic was the intense embarrassment and shame I felt over my reactions. I felt like a freak. Like a coward. I would often beg my mom or dad to stay with me. If not, I would absolutely refuse to go to an activity. I couldn't explain why I felt in danger in these situations. I felt like a burden to my family. One summer when visiting my grandparents, I remember pleading with my parents to let us kids sleep with them in our trailer, parked in the driveway, instead of sleeping overnight in the house. I was told that it would hurt my grandma's feelings if we didn't sleep in her house, which just proved to me I was being selfish.

I reasoned that my fears were bizarre and I was interfering with the lives I so admired. With four kids and a full schedule, our family was busy, and frankly there wasn't time to put up with my demands for special treatment, especially when I couldn't articulate why I was so desperate to not be away from them. I only had fragments of frightening images associated with these places, and I couldn't make sense of them myself. Many years would pass before repressed memories would fully surface—that I had been sexually abused as a child when my parents weren't with me. It would be a long time before those fragments came together and I understood how profoundly those situations affected me.

> My sense of failure and feelings of shame were offset by packing my days with activities.

Until then, shame and a creeping sense of danger simply became my daily companions. I had learned that the way it worked was to "fear not" because God would always take care of me. But I couldn't seem to help being afraid—sometimes terrified—so in my young mind, I was failing miserably at what I most wanted to be—a good daughter and a good Christian.

My sense of failure and feelings of shame were offset by packing my days with activities. I excelled at academics and devoured books in my free time. Often in my bedroom I would hear my mom calling me from another part of the house, and I would frustrate her to no end by diving behind my bed just to read a few more pages. Making friends came easily for me, so I had plenty of relationships to distract me. Endless hours were spent playing the piano and singing and harmonizing with my sister. Our family was active; and I loved gymnastics, roller skating, any outdoor game, and especially horseback riding. Hands down, my happiest childhood memories are from our time spent at a Rocky Mountain dude ranch. Our family vacationed there one glorious week every summer, and we rode horses and ate gourmet meals to our hearts' content. Busy with these activities, I would lose myself and temporarily forget about the phobias, nightmares, and shame.

Besides the violent night terrors and daytime fears, one other area of perceived failure plagued me with confusion. I felt like I just wasn't measuring up in the eyes of my older brother, who was just two years older than me. Steve and I were close and played together easily when we were young children. I looked up to him for a lot of reasons but mainly because he was fun, fearless, and really, really smart. He learned to read when he was two-and-a-half years old and was scouring the newspaper before leaving for kindergarten at the ripe age of four. As he moved into middle and high school, he became increasingly moody, withdrawn, and often angry. Steve was a freethinker, developing his own ideas about the world as he gathered information and took in a global perspective. His ideas didn't gel with the conservative viewpoint at home or with the teachers at the small private school we attended.

By this time in my life so much of my identity was dependent on other people that I had developed a hyper-vigilant awareness of the feelings and opinions of those around me. This is the heart of codependency, needing others to be OK so I can be OK. Steve's approval mattered deeply to me, and I internalized every "bad day" or frustration of his as somehow being directed toward me. What I didn't know then was that most of the time the people around me aren't thinking about me at all—they're thinking about themselves!

Unknown to me, struggles with substance abuse had started to get a grip on my brother. As often happens when someone gets caught in a cycle of substance dependence, his personality started to undergo drastic swings. I never knew "which" Steve to expect on any given day. Maybe he'd be mellow and want to hang out and play card games like Pit or spoons. Maybe he'd crack jokes that made us hold our sides laughing. Or would he come home and yank me out of the chair closest to the TV, demanding his spot? Or ignore me completely and retreat to his basement room, slamming the door behind him? My thinking was so distorted by this time that I was convinced his behavior was a reflection of what he thought about me. I just wanted to hang out with him and couldn't understand why we fought so much.

Of course, on top of it all, I was an emotional teenage girl. It seemed like other brothers and sisters got along great, so what was wrong with us? I had no real data to go on, just my own *Little House on the Prairie*–style fantasy of how life should be. I saw life in black and white, all or nothing.

Steve graduated before my sophomore year, and I made a major change myself, leaving the small private school and attending the local high school to be part of the gymnastics team. It was quite the adjustment going from a class of twenty-five students to a student body of several thousand! The following year we moved to the Northwest, leaving Steve behind and putting more than a thousand miles between us. My new school was a third of the size of the one I'd attended my sophomore year, which opened up more opportunities to participate in activities. I threw myself into as many things as I could: band, choir, gymnastics, running the school store, National

Honor Society, private music lessons, and church, to name a few. The busier I was the better I felt! Or rather, the less I felt.

Nightmares and fears of being abandoned still plagued me, but I was sophisticated enough by this time to keep those under wraps most of the time. I managed—which is very different from actually living. I still look back with regret on how much I missed out on by "managing." My junior year the King Tut exhibit made a rare stop in Seattle, and I desperately wanted to see it; although I was seventeen by then, anxiety about getting separated from the group and risking a panic attack trumped that unique opportunity. Managing fear is exhausting! It's also riddled with disappointments and missed opportunities.

> You never know what might be waiting for you just around the corner.

I had resigned myself to a life of maneuvering to avoid panic. I saw no way out. But you never know what might be waiting for you just around the corner—an encounter, an event, an idea—something that might just break you free and steer you back toward the person you were born to be. The summer before I moved away for college, an unexpected experience ignited fresh revelation in the darkness that haunted my daily life. Just after sunrise, sitting on the shore of a picturesque lake, I breathed the still air, drank in the beauty of the pine trees and quiet water, and talked to God. I talked to God with a soul full of shame. The evening before in the light of a blazing bonfire, a group of friends and I had roasted s'mores, sung along with a guitar, and talked late into the night. The pickup truck that had driven us the short distance through the woods from the cabin a few hours earlier was heading back. We had the option to ride back or linger by the fire and walk back. Everyone wanted to stay. And so did I, but once again panic started to rise. The thought of getting lost in the dark, unfamiliar woods closed my throat up with fear. Heart racing, I opted to ride back.

Thinking about it the in the light of day, I loathed myself. I felt completely enslaved by fear. So I repeatedly apologized to God about feeling afraid. I was sure that God was just as disgusted with me as I was. Usually these conversations were one-sided. Often I was so engrossed in telling God my faults and asking for forgiveness that I left no time to receive any insight. I had heard that prayer is talking to God and meditation is listening—well, I was too busy talking to try the meditation thing. But that morning was different. Very clearly I sensed a question coming back at me: Kathy, are you going to turn your fears over to me?

I was so stunned I could barely breathe. I intuitively knew that what I was sensing was real. And that left me in a sweaty dilemma. The impression was so strong I knew I was being nudged to make a decision. My instinct was to shrink back and say no. Once again, I was afraid. If I said yes, what if it didn't help? After all, God is the last house on the block, and if He couldn't fix me, I was screwed. After what seemed like an hour of debating in my mind, I made a decision. I chose yes. I said yes in my spirit, and I meant it. I responded with my will and with my heart, but I had no clue if it would make any difference.

Incredibly, something lifted that morning. My life was different after that. Although my nights were still plagued with terrifying dreams, during my waking hours I had no conscious fear. Even better, no panic attacks. The relief was incredible. The freedom was like nothing I'd ever experienced! I couldn't believe it. This was God doing for me what I could not do for myself.

Even though Lisa and I never knew Dr. Bernard Nathanson personally, he understood our confusion; like Lisa's, his childhood was based on ethics and morality that were constantly changing as he witnessed wrong being perceived as right. Like me, in a family chock full of intellectual achievers, Bernie sought approval through intellectual accomplishments. All three of us were derailed in childhood only to be restored later in life. What was the common force that eventually restored us to our original destiny? The thread that weaves our divine purpose together?

LISA'S
Liberation

"You've Come a Long Way, Baby."

~Virginia Slims Cigarette Slogan

The 1970s were all about fun and exploration. It was the time of bell bottoms, 8-track tapes, lava lamps, waterbeds, and Watergate. Self-fulfillment, freedom, and equality were the prevailing philosophy. The Vietnam War was coming to an end, and people were about "making love, not war." Technology was on the rise, and we were newly bombarded with feminist messages like "You've come a long way, baby" and "I can bring home the bacon, fry it up in the pan." Farrah Fawcett, Donna Summer, and Linda Evans were icons molding female fashion, while Gloria Steinem and Betty Friedan were expanding the second wave of the feminist culture and Helen Reddy was singing the women's national anthem "I Am Woman." The women's rights movement was in full bloom. Feminists of the movement declared that they would revolutionize the way women were treated and identified by society. Aspiring to empower, the movement urged women to engage in the pursuit of higher education and to strive for careers that would break the stereotypes of the time. Driven by the sexual revolution, the hippie subculture, and the thrust of the civil rights movement, public consciousness was shifting.

My father, an avid reader, had a great interest in politics and current events. *Time, Newsweek,* and the *Washington Post* were regularly delivered to our home; and the eleven o'clock news was a weeknight tradition. Although neither sex nor abstinence was ever discussed in my home, the subject did crop up in the media coverage of the day. Because of this, I was aware of political and legislative news as well as social developments.

In the late 1960s and early 1970s women were limited to chart very few courses: get married, have children; and be a housewife; or become a teacher, nurse, or secretary. Drastic changes in perceptions were arising, and women wanted to spread their wings and fly. Feminism had become the little engine that could. Headlining the nightly news was the women's liberation movement. It was a united struggle for equality—a series of crusades and reforms on issues such as equal pay, domestic violence, maternity leave, sexual harassment, and women's health. Great strides were made that foreshadowed the Rachael Rays and Condoleezza Rices of today.

It was a time that ushered in some much-needed changes that we take for granted today. But along with the good came a lot of the bad. On the one hand was the notion that women actually had sexual desires that needed to be met; on the other was a growing acceptance of premarital sex. Feminists claimed that the sexual revolution was vital to the women's movement, declaring that single women had the right to the same sexual freedoms as single men. This philosophy was supported by the availability of the birth control pill in the late 1960s, which allowed sexual encounters free from the worry of pregnancy.

I never really thought too much about sex until the summer of 1973. I was fourteen years old and had already been drunk several times. I had even tried pot and liked it. That summer I noticed that guys were looking at me differently. They seemed more interested. I felt special, attractive, powerful, and free, especially in the context of shameful feelings that I had been harboring about myself since I was five. So when Billy, the handsome, seventeen-year-old lifeguard showed an interest in me, I was ecstatic! On our first "date," which wasn't anything more than a ride home, we smoked a joint and I surrendered. This was the summer I lost my virginity, in the backseat of Billy's bright orange mustang. I was a "grown woman" at last.

Changing times and conditions created conflict that wasn't dissipating.

How girls love to talk! By my own choice, I was attending La Reine, an all-girls Catholic high school run by the Bernardine Sisters. It may seem odd that I chose to attend such a strict, authoritarian school, but my other option was Suitland High School. School desegregation in Prince George's County, Maryland, began in 1973 when I was attending public junior high. Changing times and conditions created conflict that wasn't dissipating. By the end of my ninth-grade year at Francis Scott Key Junior High, I was tired of the chaos and wanted to go to school in peace. Having friends that were attending Suitland High and hearing about the tense atmosphere, as well as the number of fights and assaults, I pleaded with my parents to send me to La Reine, and my request was granted.

Catholic school provided an atmosphere of camaraderie balanced with great standards of discipline. They strived to create students with high moral values through obedience and uniformity. You could spot a girl who attended La Reine a mile away. In the warmer months we wore short-waisted, knee-length, pastel cotton dresses; in the winter, a plaid, pleated skirt with a matching powder-blue wool blazer. Uniforms were a tool to create conformity, but my longing was for my own authenticity. If being the "real me" meant rebelling against conventional thinking, so be it. Secretly, I knew that there were others who gained belonging through rebellion.

My afternoon English literature class was taught by Ms. Jefferson—a trendy and fashionable '70s kind of gal. Not only was Ms. Jefferson beautiful, she was outrageously hip and refreshingly progressive; I just loved her class! We always seemed to get off topic and have totally open-minded discussions—so cool. During one of our "off the cuff" discussions, a classmate mentioned a book her older sister was reading about female sexuality entitled *The Hite Report*. The author interviewed a thousand women aged fourteen to sixty and asked them questions about sex, then went on to dispel the myths and encourage women's sexual activity.

> Secretly, I knew that there were others who gained belonging through rebellion.

That night I went out, bought the book, and began reading. The author encouraged female sexual freedom, an opinion I agreed with. This book also discussed the use of the birth-control pill, a subject much read about and talked about among my "grown-up," cool friends. These girls told me that if you went to your doctor and told him you suffered from difficult periods and severe menstrual cramps you could land a prescription. They were right. I was able to convince my gynecologist that due to serious problems with my period, I needed to be put on "the pill." Dr. Provos, who smoked cigarettes the entire time I sat in his office for consultation, never warned me about any side effects of "the pill"; in fact he never even mentioned that its purpose was for birth control. Gosh, I loved that doctor! He prescribed the birth-control pill, which gave me the ability to engage in as much sex as I wanted without a thought of getting pregnant. Needless to say, the time I spent with Billy increased dramatically! Figuring out ways to have "alone" time with him consumed much of my thinking.

During another class discussion, the topic of abortion arose. We all agreed that the government and male politicians should not tell a woman what to do with her body and that it is a "woman's right to choose." After all, I did watch the nightly news and even read top news magazines. This gave me the courage to openly share that I was in favor of choice and the medical procedure of abortion. Women needed to have freedom. Even Ms. Jefferson was in agreement.

During my last year of high school, I had the opportunity to take part in a school program called career scheduling. This meant I attended school half a day and worked in the afternoon, which counted as class credit. I quickly landed a job in a bank, and not long after my first paycheck I decided that higher education wasn't for me. It couldn't hold a candle to the freedom and independence of being a working woman, earning money, and living on my own. This newfound destiny was also a vehicle to meet more progressive, beautiful people.

Soon I met the man of my dreams, or so I thought. He was a gorgeous Latino man, seventeen years my senior, and shortly after meeting him we were engaged. But like so much in my life, this relationship was a dream of what I wanted my life to be. Like a chameleon, I dove into the Hispanic culture, loving every aspect of its diversity. My fiancé wore fancy clothes and took me to fine restaurants where we drank rare wine and liquor. We would top off the evening by returning to his apartment for a night of uninhibited sex. This relationship proved to be an aphrodisiac to the lifestyle I wanted to live. This was a life that would provide equality, fulfillment, power, and fun. However, after discovering that he owed child support and was on the verge of being unemployed I ran for the hills.

With a broken engagement under my belt, I moved on. As I began to experience this next newfound independence I soon realized that I was actually happy. I was a survivor. Leaving behind the "socially backward thinking" of the Catholic hierarchy and fully embracing the '70s enlightenment doctrine, I believed that freedom would ultimately bring greater satisfaction than being married and tied down. After all, I was woman. I was invincible.

BERNIE

Becomes a Doctor

"People who lean on logic and philosophy
and rational exposition end
by starving the best part of the mind."

~WILLIAM BUTLER YEATS

On a hot August day in 1943, Bernie walked onto the campus
at Cornell University and breathed in the air of independence.
He was seventeen years old, and a big world was opening for
him to conquer! Before leaving home, Bernie took his courageous stand against Joseph, refusing to denigrate his mother
any longer. He had rejected the role of surrogate assassin. For
the first time, freedom to be his own man was possible. Hope
soared with a college career at his fingertips, one that held the
promise of leading to a prestigious medical school. Here he
could feed his insatiable hunger for knowledge. As classes com-
menced, he kept his head low, stuck to his schoolwork, and
spent his nights playing poker with a few friends. Not exactly
what most of us would call living it up, but for Bernie it was
sweet liberty.

During his undergrad days World War II was in a climactic shift, and Bernie was itching to get in on the action. Joseph Nathanson, on the other hand, adamantly opposed a military career for his son. At the beginning of his sophomore year, Bernie was ecstatic when he got his notice from Uncle Sam to appear for his mandatory military physical. It was a kick in the gut when he was given a 4-F deferment, "unfit for military service" due to his mildly poor eyesight. But when his friend with terrible vision was enlisted without hesitation, Bernie was confused—and suspicious. Somehow, he knew, his dad had interfered. Just when he finally thought he was free, his all-controlling father crushed his dreams once more. Humiliated but powerless to change the situation, Bernie let resentment over being manipulated smolder in his chest. But a slow-burning resentment left unchecked will consume and morph a soul into the very thing it despises. Without knowing it, Bernie was germinating the seeds of becoming a master manipulator himself.

Bernie finished his undergraduate studies with blistering speed. Under his father's direction he applied to both Harvard and McGill for medical school. Bernie was rejected by both. He had emerged from his pre-med studies with merely average grades. Could this have anything to do with the fact that he crammed a four-year degree into two years? Joseph Nathanson seethed. His well-laid plans for his only son, an extension of himself wouldn't go up in smoke. Bernie wouldn't go into the military, and he wouldn't go down in shame, either. Not on his watch. Planning ahead, he had already greased the skids for his son by manipulating a friendship with one of the leading faculty members at McGill. The man was a heavy drinker, and for several years Joseph had periodically invited him out for a night of carousing. Joseph himself rarely drank, so these nights would end in the wee hours of the morning with two results: the noose slipped a little tighter around the McGill pawn and Joseph puking his guts out on the curb in front his home. But the payoff was worth it. The brilliant manipulator timed his phone call expressing his outrage just when his inebriated friend would be at his weakest. And voilà! A spot opened up for Bernie at McGill.

> A slow-burning resentment left unchecked will consume and morph a soul into the very thing it despises.

In the summer of 1945, at the age of nineteen, Bernie ventured to McGill University in a swelteringly hot Montreal, Quebec, for his first semester of doctoral studies. Here his college experience was entirely different than at Cornell. At McGill his social life thrived. Bernie ate his meals at a large boarding house with a dozen or more fellow medical students. He'd hang out with his new buddies for hours, smoking cigarettes on the patio and discussing current issues. Now this was really living! At school he was much more engaged. He took a genuine interest in his professors and befriended many of them. And by far his favorite professor was Dr. Karl Stern.

A German-born Jew with his doctorate in psychiatry, Karl Stern commanded the respect of his students—respect earned not through intimidation or the intellectual battery Bernie's father had dished out. A brilliant teacher, Stern kept his students riveted through his knowledge and innovative ideas. He taught with authority while creating an atmosphere of dignity that included everyone in the room. Bernie shadowed the man, hanging on his every word, absorbing like a sponge. When he was in Dr. Stern's presence he experienced something entirely foreign to him—he felt peace. With Karl Stern, this love-starved, resentment-riddled young man could be himself and ask questions without fear of ridicule. He could share his thoughts and have them dignified and considered. Here was a true father figure, someone without ulterior motives who was genuinely concerned for his welfare as a whole person. Bernie was nurtured intellectually and emotionally. Hanging out with Dr. Stern, Bernie felt loved. This was a far cry from the pressure to carry on the legacy of a narcissistic father. Even so, little did Bernie know how profoundly Stern would come to impact his life.

Because of Dr. Stern, Bernie threw himself into his psychiatric studies and earned the top award in that department his senior year. Much to Bernie's surprise, this beloved professor encouraged him to apply for the coveted residency in psychiatry. But Bernie turned it down and followed in his father's footsteps, pursuing obstetrics and gynecology. Perhaps deep down he was still hoping to gain his father's approval. How different Bernie's life might have been if he had accepted the residency and remained under the influence of Karl Stern! But years later Dr. Stern would resurface in his life. Serving as a wise mentor, he would lead Bernie to that same peace he had tasted years before.

At McGill, Bernie was first indoctrinated with the mindset of the superiority of a physician over his patient. It was universally assumed that the doctor was always right; and the patient was expected to follow his orders, no questions asked. This was the 1940s, an era of physicians in a god-like role. For Bernie, it was a soothing balm to a bruised ego, to one dominated so completely in his childhood.

True to his sensitive nature he was genuinely concerned for the welfare of the patient. He was in the business to help people. But one encounter sealed this "Doctor knows best" conviction in him, which would fuel much of his mentality in the years to come. While shadowing a resident physician on the gynecology ward, he witnessed the aftermath of a suspected abortion—illegal at the time. A woman was bleeding heavily and screaming from excruciating pain. She claimed she was having a miscarriage. The police elbowed the physicians aside and interrogated the woman for an absurd amount of time before finally allowing her to be treated. Bernie was appalled by the intrusion of the law, ignoring the obvious suffering of the patient! What was wrong with them; how could they be so cruel? Couldn't they see this woman was in severe pain?

This picture of injustice toward women was seared into Bernie's mind. This brought flashbacks of the injustice suffered by his mother in her own home. The mistreatment of this disadvantaged patient ignited a passion in him to help women in dire circumstances. Bernie began to see the law against abortion as an obstacle to a woman's health. But just around the bend, another experience would deeply impact his convictions. Abortion was about to get up close and personal.

His first autumn at McGill, Bernie and a group of buddies attended a campus dance. Across the packed dance floor a beautiful coed caught his eye. Wasting no time he maneuvered through the crowd and asked her to dance. Mesmerized by the beautiful Russian Jewish girl, he couldn't believe his good fortune to find her captivating, innocent, and extremely intelligent. He had hit the jackpot! Ruth Potemkin was a freshman studying at the Royal Victoria College, and Bernie fell head over heels. They began spending all their free hours together and in no time were swept up in an all-consuming romance. Before long they were sleeping together. Their relationship was passionate, loving, and carefree. Three beautiful years later they were still going strong, and Ruth and Bernie were seriously discussing marriage.

And then Ruth suspected she was pregnant. All of a sudden the warmth and hope for a future seemed to drain out of their relationship. Bernie panicked and reverted to what was familiar, and what had worked for him in the past. He contacted his father. Joseph tested Ruth's urine, and the lab results confirmed that Ruth was pregnant. He wrote his son a letter that detailed only two options: Ruth needed to have an abortion, or Bernie needed to marry her. The letter included $500 for the abortion. In other words, "Ride out the storm or jump ship. Here's your life raft."

Our limited experience narrows our world, conceals other alternatives, and constricts our hearts.

Without warning Bernie's consuming passion for Ruth took a backseat to his career ambitions. He had a year and a half of medical studies left and another five to six years of residency training. The idea of marriage, so enticing only months before, morphed into an ugly liability. In an amazing example of perception determining reality, Bernie convinced himself that terminating the pregnancy was the only option. In our lives we have so many options, but our limited experience narrows our world, conceals other alternatives, and constricts our hearts. As Bernie himself said later in life, he "craved love—and then perverted it."[1] He considered only the options that were self-serving.

As a medical student Bernie was all too aware of the dangers abortions posed to women. Because it was illegal, he also knew that if he was involved in any way in Ruth's abortion, it could mean a setback in his career. All practicing doctors then and today recite the Hippocratic Oath, and in the 1940s and '50s there was a section that spoke directly of abortions: "I will give no deadly medicine to anyone if asked, nor suggest any such counsel; and in like manner I will not give to a woman a pessary [a device inserted in the vagina thought, erroneously, to initiate an abortion] to produce an abortion."[2]

He found a doctor willing to carry out the termination, and Ruth made an appointment. The night before the procedure, they held each other and wept for their unborn child. Would things ever be the same after this loss? The next day they agreed to meet on the library steps when the abortion was done. Bernie fretfully paced while he waited. At dusk her cab pulled up, four hours late, and Bernie carried beautiful Ruth, pale and crying inconsolably, out of the cab. All that was left of their child was a pool of blood on the floorboard of the taxi.

Sitting on the steps of the library in the gathering darkness, Bernie cradled Ruth and they sobbed together again. She muttered Russian prayers in between her falling tears. Putting her in a car he had borrowed, he drove her to her parents' house and nursed her for two nights. Surprisingly she was able to return to class. Bernie knew the questions that plagued Ruth's thoughts: Why didn't he marry me? Why couldn't we have had this baby? Will God punish me for what I have done by making me barren?

Bernie, on the other hand, wasn't concerned about God. What did God have to do with this? His mind was burdened with only two thoughts: Would she fully recover physically, and would she give him the same carefree love she had before? One was the question of a concerned physician, the other a question of a self-centered heart. Ruth did recover quickly, physically at least, but the spark in her eyes and in their love affair had grown dim. They slept together only once more, a passionless and impersonal encounter. Their relationship had been permanently altered, and Bernie and Ruth parted ways. Bernie didn't know then how deeply he would regret the loss of this beautiful, loving woman and their child in the years to come.

But life moved on without Ruth; and on a hazy June morning in 1949, Bernie took his Hippocratic Oath and graduated as Dr. Bernard Nathanson. He relocated to Chicago, where he entered his first residency at Michael Reese Hospital. This Jewish hospital was known for its excellence but definitely not for its ethics. As he worked alongside these physicians, Dr. Nathanson witnessed the twisted morals they regularly practiced without batting an eyelash. Bernie had been subjected to many lectures by his father on the evils of unethical practices in medicine. But he was astonished when he actually saw rampant unnecessary surgeries, fee-splitting, and kickbacks. This was Bernie's foundation in the "real world" of doctoring. Although his father was corrupt in his personal life, he was meticulously ethical in his professional life. Once again Bernie was conflicted. Could this mean his father had been right all along? A shift was taking place in him. His moral compass was becoming skewed and unreliable.

Following his Michael Reese residency, Dr. Bernard Nathanson took a position at New York Hospital. Looking for love in all the "right" places, he met his first wife at the hospital. It was a match made in heaven, or so it seemed. On the surface they were perfect for each other. They were both doctors, both Jewish, and both raised in the same anemic spiritual atmosphere. Digging deeper, however, they found they had little in common and even less passion. Bernie never felt strongly committed to his marriage and calculated that if things didn't work out he would simply file for divorce. A mentality of disposable lives began to seem natural and logical.

Moving on to the prestigious Women's Hospital of New York in 1952, Bernie had only been married a short time but already was dissatisfied. He started hatching an escape plan. The following year he enlisted in the Air Force and was stationed in St. John's, Newfoundland, where he practiced gynecology. Built on a shallow foundation, Bernie knew that the marriage wouldn't survive the separation and change; in fact, he counted on it. Divorce papers were drawn up as soon as he returned to New York. The marriage had lasted only four and a half years. They parted civilly, and Dr. Nathanson never saw his first wife again. His heart was becoming increasingly detached by his self-serving decisions. Bernie already had two failed relationships under his belt, and they wouldn't be the last.

As Kathy would learn to do years later, Bernie crammed his schedule full, leaving little time to feel. During his grueling residency at the Women's Hospital, he worked thirty-six-hour shifts that often included a late night call to the emergency room to treat patients suffering complications from illegally performed abortions. Often black or Puerto Rican, these underprivileged women wailed in agony as they hemorrhaged what was left of their unborn child. Botched abortions in this era often led to raging fevers, torn intestines, bleeding out, abscesses, an emergency hysterectomy, and even sterilization. No wonder he was upset.

> A mentality of disposable lives began to seem natural and logical.

Bernie's passion for safe medical treatment for women was growing into a consuming fire in the early 1950s. He began to observe an alarming difference between the wealthy and the poor. The poorer women weren't there because they were suffering from a common cold. For something as serious as abortion, this was a huge inequity. In private practice wealthy women were given attentive physical care and treated with dignity. In comparison, underprivileged and minority women received impersonal, disinterested treatment following abortions initiated at home or at some shady, unsanitary practice.

Dr. Nathanson grew more and more disgusted as he stood by helplessly watching the vastly different treatment given to the women in these two socioeconomic classes. By word of mouth, he found a doctor in Puerto Rico, Juan Rodriguez, and enthusiastically began referring his pregnant patients to him so they could have "safe" and legal abortions. Soon ninety percent of the Puerto Rican doctor's business came from the east coast of the United States, and he amassed a fortune. Nathanson had spoken to the affluent doctor many times on the phone but had never met him in person. So, when on a long layover in San Juan, on a whim, Bernie decided to drop by his colleague's clinic and meet him face to face.

Catching a taxi he arrived at the grey stucco building that housed the practice, walked in, and introduced himself. He was immediately taken aback at the cramped facility that serviced an enormous number of patients. He noticed with alarm no receptionist or nurse. In fact, Rodriguez was the only one at the clinic: employer and employee in one. But he had a confident manner and spoke excellent English. Besides, he had numerous diplomas displayed behind his desk, which put Nathanson's mind at ease. That is, until he saw the procedure room. It had two large open windows at street level where passersby were stopping to say hello to the doctor. He then saw the poor excuse for an operating table that, to his horror, allowed Rodriguez to administer anesthesia himself and then rush to the other end, put the patient's feet in the stirrups, and perform the procedure. He was a one-man band, with no backup in case of complications.

Rodriguez picked up on Nathanson's alarm and hurried to show him his many diplomas. On closer scrutiny, it was obvious that each one had been purchased! Even after this incredible shock, Nathanson failed to step back and reevaluate. He continued referring women to Puerto Rico for abortions until he was presented with another option. Once he met Dr. Milan Vuitch, a practicing abortionist, he began referring his patients to Vuitch's clinic located in Washington, DC.

Bernie's passion for providing safe medical care for women became an obsession with abortion. The reasons women sought abortion weren't important to Bernie. He never even considered providing alternatives such as adoption or temporary foster care to women who wanted to end their pregnancy. All moral conviction he possessed was focused solely on solving one dilemma: finding a way for women to terminate their unwanted pregnancies safely. He was absolutely determined to find ways around the law.

One fateful night in 1967 at a dinner party given by a colleague, the volatile substances of intellect and conviction combined to create a mechanism that would soon unleash an explosion of abortion law reform to sweep over an unsuspecting nation.

BERNIE

Dark World of Abortion—
Dawn of Awakening

"A liar begins with making falsehood appear like truth,
and ends with making truth itself appear like falsehood."

~WILLIAM SHENSTONE

What we do with our lives matters. Regardless of what you do, you matter. Whether your focus is reaching out to the less fortunate, breaking down racial barriers, changing local or national policy, or simply working to put food on the table, you matter. Just a mom or dad in a dead-end job? You are impacting multiple future generations with your efforts and your attitude! Single and maybe working in sales, administration, or business and just looking for a good time on the weekends? You matter. In college, slugging it out semester after semester to earn that degree? You influence, for better or for worse, everyone you come in contact with.

And who we hang around with matters. It's a choice we make. It doesn't "just happen." Put another way, as Kathy's father-in-law always says, "*Who* you associate with is as important as what you *believe.*" *Who* Bernie Nathanson ended up associating with mattered—a lot. In fact, it's not an exaggeration to say that one relationship changed an entire nation.

It was the late '60s, and Dr. Bernard Nathanson's career was in full swing. His second wife, Rosemary, had given him a biography of James Joyce; and wouldn't you know, like father like son, Bernie became an obsessed fan of one historical figure. For his father, it had been Abraham Lincoln; for Bernie, it was James Joyce. When he wasn't working long hours at the Women's Hospital or in his private practice or teaching at Cornell Medical School, he was devouring everything he could find on James Joyce. So when he was invited to a dinner party with other Joyce enthusiasts he jumped at the chance. Although operating in extremes with a self-induced twenty-four-hour packed schedule, he definitely found time to squeeze this in. By this time Bernie had divorced Rosemary and married his third wife, Adelle.

It was June of 1967. As Bernie sat down to the dinner table, he was introduced to the gentleman seated next to him, Lawrence Lader. He didn't give him a second thought, but as Bernie turned away to talk with another guest, Lader made a passing comment about just having published a book titled *Abortion.* That's all it took. If there was one subject Bernie was more passionate about than James Joyce, it was abortion.

The two quickly became close friends, and their conversations always found their way around to their favorite subject: abortion law reform. At last, Bernie's need to be needed, his love-starved ache to be valued was being met. Larry Lader was a wealthy socialite-turned-journalist; and early in his adult life he worked for Vito Marcantonio, the only card-carrying communist ever elected to congress. Lader fell in love with revolutionary thinking and anything he considered social injustice. He had just written a biography with and about Margaret Sanger, who was the godmother of American eugenics: the study of creating the perfect race by encouraging the reproduction of people with desirable traits and discouraging or even preventing the reproduction of people with less than desirable traits. As intellectual elitists, both Sanger and Lader thought they could be judge and jury over who had value.

Feminism was the latest and greatest movement that fit into his radical thinking. Although Lader *fought* for feminist causes, Bernie would later describe the man who was to become his best friend as an absolute chauvinist in his own home.[1] He talked a good game about betterment for the poor and disenfranchised, but he lived a lavish lifestyle and kept his distance from anyone actually in that category. It was revolutionary fervor he was enamored with, not people. Manipulating the masses and radical change are what got Lader out of bed in the morning.

Bernie, on the other hand, was passionate about the abortion issue because he genuinely agonized over the plight of the poor woman who found herself "unwillingly pregnant." Daily, desperate women were coming to him for care, many of them suffering from botched abortions. Exactly how to right this wrong was constantly working in his mind—the mind of a man whose society reinforced the god complex physicians were encouraged to adopt.

Thus one man, driven by outrage over appalling healthcare for women, would do whatever it took to resolve what he saw as a huge injustice in the face of the laws of the day. It never entered his mind how abortion could affect the fathers of those babies, the unborn children themselves, or even the women, after the fact. Living in extremes can do that, showing us things in black and white, preventing us from considering other perspectives. Operating on autopilot, he never questioned his solution: unlimited, affordable access to abortion on demand was the only answer.

And so the two zealots began plotting their revolution. Actually, it was more like Nathanson was swept up by Lader and enlisted as his right-hand man before he even realized what was happening. Lisa is kind of like Lader in Kathy's life. They share similar passions, and Lisa is the one to throw her arm around Kathy's shoulders and say, "Hey, you won't believe where we're going next! It's going to be great!" One major difference, however— Lisa is no elitist but is genuinely concerned about the welfare of others.

> Every movement needs a villain.

Larry and Bernie would retreat to a beautiful beach home on the island of St. Croix for a month at a time to relax in the sun, eat delicious meals, drink, and strategize. It was there that Larry drilled him on the basics of revolutionary politics. The first priority was to create publicity. They would mesmerize the public with demonstrations, disruption, and lawsuits. Lader emphasized the importance of ruthlessly courting the press and TV, especially flattering the female reporters. The message the public would repeatedly hear was "We're here, we're watching, we're powerful, and we're angry!" If they had the press on their side, even a small minority would appear to be a massive number of Americans, which still holds true today. He insisted on keeping the women out front, especially black women. In one subsequent demonstration, his strategy was to have women pushing baby carriages in the lead, loudly chanting slogans.

But every movement needs a villain. In this case, the perfect fit was the Catholic hierarchy. Although it was the American Medical Association that had influenced anti-abortion laws, not the Catholic leaders, facts didn't drive this campaign; perception did.[2] They painted their bull's-eye on the leaders only, not on the masses of Roman Catholics. They were selling to a culture obsessed with the sexual revolution, and the Vatican had stringent standards on birth control and sex.

Their goal was national abortion law reform, and the linchpin was to take down the current New York state abortion restrictions. If they accomplished that, New York City would become the "abortion capitol of the East," and Lader and Nathanson would be in the driver's seat leading the way for the rest of the nation. They organized a conference in Chicago in 1969 for national leaders in the pro-abortion movement. From that meeting the National Association for Repeal of Abortion Laws, NARAL, was birthed. Although women were named as president and vice president, Lader was the real authority behind their decisions. He was the puppet master pulling the strings.

A central and repeated tactic was to feed false polls, and outright lies, to the media. They had as an ally a renowned bio-statistician, Dr. Christopher Tietze, a silent co-conspirator in the widespread deception, who never denied what he knew to be false.[3]

In his article *Confessions of an Ex-Abortionist*, Nathanson wrote, "We persuaded the media that the cause of permissive abortion was a liberal enlightened, sophisticated one. Knowing that if a true poll were taken, we would be soundly defeated, we simply fabricated the results of fictional polls. We announced to the media that we had taken polls and that 60% of Americans were in favor of permissive abortion. This is the tactic of the self-fulfilling lie. Few people care to be in the minority."[4]

One statistic Nathanson later admitted was an outright lie was the one mentioned earlier: that ten thousand women in America died each year from botched abortions, when the reality was around 200–250. That is only two percent of their claim![5] They fabricated a poll, one they had never actually taken, claiming that "most" rational Americans were already on board with abortion on demand. The press ate it up and beat the drum loudly and repeatedly. It's similar to the tactics of tobacco companies who advertise the benefits of smoking even though they have evidence of its harmful effects.

Effective on July 1, 1970, passing by only one vote, the New York state bill allowing abortion on demand up to the twenty-fourth week of pregnancy was signed into law. To stage more media hype, Nathanson held a symposium on abortion technique on that same day. Even though only eighty doctors attended, a negligible number, the massive media coverage gave the impression that all of the major medical societies were represented and in agreement. In reality, the medical establishment was not in agreement and did everything in its power to limit the number of hospital beds available for abortions.

As predicted, New York was inundated with women from all over the East Coast wanting to end their unwanted pregnancies. Bernie had a tiger by the tail now that abortion was legalized. He worked himself to the bone making sure abortion would be practical and available to everyone. His life was spinning out of control as chairman of the Medical Committee of NARAL, setting up ambulatory abortion clinics and inspecting existing (previously illegal) abortion clinics for safety. In addition, he was acting as the senior member of a busy OB/GYN group at St. Luke's Women's Hospital, and as Chief of Gynecology at the Hospital for Joint Diseases. This was a man who couldn't say no—and his life was about to get even busier.

Enter the Reverend Howard Moody, another key player in the game for revolutionary social change. Leading the congregants of the Judson Memorial Church and founding their nonprofit Center for Reproductive and Sexual Health (CRASH), Moody wielded powerful influence in New York City. His country manners and good old boy charm were the perfect cover for his iron rule through intimidation. But he had a big problem on his hands. His clinic was only days from being shut down for dismal substandard practices.

Bernie was the perfect target for the slick, manipulative, and prestigious reverend. Moody unexpectedly called Bernie late one evening and pleaded with him to run the non-profit abortion clinic associated with his church. He appealed to Nathanson's expertise as a doctor and his dedication to abortion. The best objection Bernie could muster was "God, Howard! God!"[6] He hung up the phone having overcommitted once again and agreed to head up the clinic for six months. That six-month commitment stretched into a year and a half of his life. It was then that Bernie became fully immersed in the grisly reality of abortion.

> Bernie was the perfect target for the slick, manipulative, and prestigious reverend.

Moody's staff was, in Nathanson's word, "deplorable." It included drunks, druggies, sadists, sexual molesters, incompetents, and plain old medical losers. One was even a fugitive from the FBI! The clinic was grossly substandard. Physicians often didn't wash their hands between abortions, didn't even sterilize their instruments. (Little did he know that fifty-seven million abortions later, unsanitary and unsterilized conditions would still be epidemic in abortion clinics.)[7]

Bernie fired most of the staff, brought in clean instruments and equipment, and hired a competent medical team. The standard of care improved, but that didn't change the grim atmosphere of the clinic. Before the law was passed, ten abortions on average were performed each day. That number rose to 120 abortions per day with the clinic hopping from 8:00 a.m. until midnight. Up until this time his focus had been on helping the few women in desperate circumstances seeking abortion. But

Bernie got caught up in the fever and began to see abortion as a numbers game. Doctors were profiting hugely from the abortion business. An average salary for a physician was $45,000 in 1970,[8] but one of the clinic's doctors netted $185,000 in a single year.[9]

During this marathon of frenzied work Dr. Nathanson presided over the termination of 75,000 lives.[10] His goal was to see every woman who walked through the clinic doors get an abortion. He went as far as to suspend a pregnant doctor, afraid that her presence might convince women not to go through with their abortion. It was an ironic move for someone supposedly championing the rights of women.

Among the many abortionists with whom Dr. Nathanson associated during this time, Milan Vuitch was the most notorious. At a time when connections and appearances were crucial, Vuitch would become a key player in the abortion propaganda game.

Wanting to keep his hands clean, the Reverend Moody insisted Bernie inspect Vuitch's operation because he wanted to refer all his patients to him. Vuitch was a celebrity. He had been arrested for illegal abortion activity several years earlier in Washington, DC, but a judge ruled in his favor. Vuitch was quoted then as saying, "This is a big step forward. Now the government lawyer will be in the position of challenging my medical position. What are the jury members going to decide when a lawyer tries to tell them that the doctor is wrong about a medical matter?"[11]

Vuitch himself was an intimidating figure. Massive in build, the fifty-year-old Serbian-American had a condescending manner, coming across as unfeeling and gruff. A decade later Mark Feldstein earned the Peabody Award for his outstanding investigative work on the questionable practices of Dr. Milan Vuitch. He reported that Vuitch's abortion clinic was operating in unsanitary conditions and that his practices were unethical. One aborted infant was born alive and subsequently died after the seventeen-year-old, late-term mother was forced out of his clinic with the abortion only partially completed. Two other women died while on his operating table. All just three blocks from the White House.

Unlike Dr. Nathanson, Dr. Vuitch was not a man in the business to help women. In fact, he was a lawsuit waiting to happen.[12] However, even after Nathanson personally witnessed the unsterile and substandard conditions of his practice, he still worked with him because Vuitch was technically the best abortionist he had ever seen. Incredibly, Vuitch's skill overrode his obvious shortcomings.

Bernie left Moody's clinic near the end of 1972, exhausted and disillusioned. He had devoted all of his time to his "grand solution" to abortion, entirely neglecting his wife and four-year-old son, Joseph. Later he described this season of his life as a delinquency, a perversion of priorities that he regretted deeply.[13] Walking out of the dark doors of the abortion mill and onto the pristine floor of the obstetrics unit at St. Luke's Hospital, he encountered a stunning new technology: the ultrasound. This new equipment was the first window illuminating the wonders of human development in the womb. "We could really see the human fetus, measure it, observe it, watch it, and indeed bond with it and love it . . . I found myself bonding with the unborn."[14] Serious doubts began to stir in Bernie's consciousness regarding what he'd been doing at the clinic. He started this journey by lying to get what he wanted. Now he wondered if what he had wanted was the biggest lie of all.

Just ten miles away, eleven-year-old Lisa had no way of knowing how much the notorious Vuitch would one day impact her own life.

10

LISA
Generation Me

"I am trying to find myself. Sometimes that's not easy."
~Marilyn Monroe

The first job I had after graduation from high school was as a clerk for the United States Department of Justice. Living three miles from the District of Columbia line sometimes felt too close and other times too far away. Gang activity and crime spilled over into our neighborhood, yet the glitz and glamour of the city was always calling. At that time I was still living with my parents and yearning to branch out on my own, so my best friend Gabi and I started planning to make it happen. A few months later, and after much coercing, my father cosigned a year's lease; and we moved to an apartment in Greenbelt, Maryland in July 1977. Gabi and I had been BFFs since second grade. She was there to witness my first kiss in the sixth grade, and I was with her when she bought her first bikini. We knew we would be perfect roommates. This is when things really started to heat up. With my own apartment, a new car, and a great job, the last thing I wanted was to be tied down, so I jumped from relationship to relationship. I dated professional athletes, entertainers, company CEOs, and police officers. Weekends consisted of trips to Ocean City, Maryland; Atlantic City, New Jersey; and the Big Apple. I was finally living!

Gabi and I spent a great deal of time at Bentley's, a neighborhood bar close to the college campus. One afternoon while sitting at the bar and after several Irish coffees, a man approached Gabi and me. When he handed us his card, I could hardly contain myself: he was a photographer for *Playboy* magazine. Gabi and I both embraced our sexuality by this point. It gave us a sense of empowerment. Once again we felt the rush of liberation and freedom surge through our beings. The man explained that the magazine was doing a feature article of the girls from the University of Maryland. Despite the fact we were not students, he was very interested in doing a photo shoot. And so we went.

Posing for nude photos brought a sense of gratification and mystique. It left us feeling assertive, attractive, and sexy—which we equated with power and popularity. We were treated very professionally; and although we were not chosen for the fall issue, we were recognized throughout the campus as potential Playmates, a title we both admired. My future held so much potential! I felt like a blank canvas waiting for strands of yarn to be woven into an intricate brocade.

I cut my teeth in the generation of the sexual revolution. It was the air I breathed, the water in which I swam. During the 1960s we had begun challenging the idea of traditional sex and marriage. Once sown, the seeds of feminism, premarital sex, and homosexuality sprouted a new morality and the growth of self-indulgence. As we moved into the 1970s and '80s, these concepts formed deep roots and the "Me Generation" emerged, producing a great harvest of Americans who were in touch with "finding themselves." We must have felt lost, because everyone was trying to find themselves. Today we would call it having an identity crisis.

New concepts and philosophies were being created and adopted. We believed that all paths to deeper fulfillment—sex, alcohol, or illegal drugs—could and should be justified. Of course, one core belief of the sexual revolution was that women enjoyed and had the same sexual needs as men and should act on them. Marvin Gaye wanted to "get it on" while the group Exile wanted "to kiss you all over" and Rod Stewart kept asking "Do you think I'm sexy?" Indoctrinated by this philosophy, many people young and old adopted this way of life. My roomie and I were living large: big hair, big cars, and most important, big parties. There was no reason for restraints, and there was no end in sight. It was sex, drugs, and rock and roll, baby!

I felt like a blank canvas waiting for strands of yarn to be woven into an intricate brocade.

Another friend and coworker, Courtney, lived with her husband, Johnny, in the condominium community adjacent to our apartment complex. They were young and newly married, and they loved to party. Johnny owned a landscaping company, and a number of really cute guys worked for him. These were guys who liked to have a good time. That's when I met Ronnie, who had the most beautiful blue eyes I had ever seen, not to mention a killer bod. He was cool, calm, and collected, and we grew close quickly. We both loved concerts, dinners, and skinny dipping and ended up dating off and on for about four months. Due to my cavalier attitude about sex, there were many nights of smoking dope, drinking, and just blacking out with Ronnie. Consequently, I forgot to take my birth-control pill. When I became pregnant, I was shocked. This was definitely not in my plan, and it would definitely compromise my freedom. What was I going to do?

Quickly, I called 411—the number for telephone information in the Dark Ages before the Internet. I heard: "Information, may I help you?" I said: "Yes, I need the phone number for an abortion clinic in DC." It was as simple as that. Bernard Nathanson's legacy in action: abortion on demand.

Moments later, I was on the line with the Laurel Clinic in Washington, DC, just blocks from the White House. With all the media exposure of *Roe v. Wade*, I knew abortion would be the answer to correct my current, unfortunate situation. Abortion would fix my problem. I didn't think I had another choice. The options of adoption or even allowing the father to raise the baby didn't enter my mind. Even if they had, we were all told then that it was just a tiny mass of tissue, a collection of cells. The receptionist at the clinic assured me this was a routine outpatient medical procedure that Dr. Milan Vuitch had performed thousands of times, that he was very experienced in the simple process. When asked how far along I was, my guess was six to eight weeks. I was told that because I had caught this early, "at just the right time," all that would be removed was a mass of tissue. She said the procedure was quick and its effects were just slight cramping and some bleeding for a few days afterward. I was also instructed to wait twenty-four hours before having sex. Not so bad. Proof of pregnancy would be validated by a simple urine test, and the fee for the entire undertaking was $175. Interestingly, cash was the only form of payment the clinic would accept.

It all seemed so easy and well thought out. The receptionist's answers made me feel this was the right thing to do. In fact, I felt lucky to have happened upon a doctor who was an expert in the field. I made the appointment. Later I would find out that I was much further along—I was actually eleven weeks pregnant. I was also about to discover that this expert's bedside manner left a lot to be desired.

Up until this time I hadn't mentioned a word about being pregnant to Ronnie; and when I did, I was the one about to be shocked and dismayed. Instead of being disappointed, Ronnie was actually happy at the prospect of being a father and moving in together. I put a stop to his "lovey-dovey" family idea at once. No way was I ready for that type of responsibility; and really, I just wasn't that into him. "I have already made an appointment for an abortion," I told him. "All I need is $175. After all, it is my body, and I have the right to make choices that affect me."

It was the new line of the day, and I had fully swallowed it. Ronnie knew he didn't have much choice in the matter. Reluctantly, sadly, he folded. Intuitively, we both knew this would probably mark the end our relationship. And, not unlike with Bernie and Ruth, it did.

With our workplace blocks from Capitol Hill, Courtney and I were very familiar with downtown DC, its traffic and lack of parking. So a few days later when she offered to drive me my appointment at the Laurel Clinic, I accepted. You would never have guessed from the outside that this place was a medical clinic. Cash in hand, and a bit apprehensive, I entered the townhouse style office in a lovely part of town. There were quite a few girls in the waiting room when I arrived, which concerned me because I knew Courtney wanted to get home before afternoon rush hour. Fortunately the whole thing went down just like the receptionist said.

I signed a few legal and medical papers. The receptionist took my $175. She handed me a small plastic cup asking for a urine sample. "Take a seat," she said. "We will be with you shortly."

Looking around I noticed no art, posters, or pictures on the wall. It looked barren and empty. Clinics today are cozier, meant to make women comfortable, but the same truth applies to the abortion procedure no matter how cozy the surroundings. Not knowing what was about to happen, I kept a jovial attitude, chatting with Courtney and becoming more and more anxious to get it over with.

I blocked out my pain by escaping into thoughts of my future.

During my initial conversation with the receptionist, I could have sworn she said I would receive general anesthesia, meaning I would be knocked out. I was wrong. However, I did receive a local anesthetic, injected around my cervix, which was *supposed* to block the pain. The injection didn't work; the cramping was searing and intense. The stark atmosphere of the procedure room was not conducive to asking questions nor was the metal table meant for comfort. I heard the nurse tell the doctor, eleven weeks gestation. There was nothing else said, there were no comforting words. In fact the only thing Vuitch, the gruff, foreign doctor, screamed at me in broken English was, "Why are you crying?"

I was vulnerable and hurting, and his abrasive manner scared me. My voice quivered as I answered, "It hurts more than I thought it would."

Vuitch's response was to bark at me again. "Stop crying! I'm almost done."

As he vigorously completed what I came there to end, I blocked out my pain by escaping into thoughts of my future. Minutes later it was over, and shortly thereafter Courtney was chauffeuring me home. Relief was what I felt. Relief that the procedure was over—as well as the pregnancy.

Usually never at a loss for words, that afternoon Courtney seemed apprehensive and quiet, as though she felt sorry for me. I almost felt as though I needed to console her in some way.

Finally, after walking me up the steps into my apartment, she asked, "Are you OK?"

"I'm a little sore, but I will be fine."

"No, I mean are you OK emotionally?"

"Of course I'm OK. Why are you asking me that?"

She said that another friend who had an abortion was depressed afterward, that it took her weeks to get over her feelings of loss. "I just want you to know I'm here if you need me."

What the heck is she talking about? Need her for what? I am relieved, not depressed.

I assured her it was nothing more than physical discomfort, it was over, and I was fine. The only thing that stirred my emotions was the way the doctor treated me. He was mean and rude. I was afraid of him and too scared to ask any questions. But it was over, time to move on. Besides, if there were any psychological concerns the nurse would have mentioned it; and surely if this process had emotional risk, the doctor's demeanor would have been different. He would have been more caring and compassionate. This was all the proof I needed that abortion was exactly what they said it was: just a simple medical procedure.

By this time it was late afternoon. I chilled out, drank a glass of wine, and got a good night's sleep. The next day was Saturday, and Gabi and I were invited to join a wealthy friend at Rosecroft Raceway for a night of drinking and gambling. Of course, we gladly accepted. Back in the saddle again and living life in the fast lane. I loved it.

I was pleased I had decided to exercise my rights, but I made myself a promise: I would not miss taking my pill, no matter what. This had been way too much of an inconvenience.

11

LISA
Life in the Big City

"A girl should be classy and fabulous."

~Coco Channel

Coco Channel said, "A girl should be classy and fabulous," and honey, I was both! Independent, powerful, and spectacularly free—that was me. Just when I thought life couldn't get any better, I was offered a position for twice my government salary as a legal secretary with a large international law firm on M Street, in the heart of the District of Columbia.

Simultaneously, Gabi's dreams were coming true as she went off to Paris on a modeling contract. Two things that didn't change were my ever-present search for identity and my curiosity. These kept me on the hunt for uncommon friends and strange bedfellows. In hopes of fulfilling this quest, I leased a beautiful efficiency apartment at DuPont Circle, which is one of DC's trendiest neighborhoods with its collection of nightclubs, bars, cafes, art galleries, and shops. It is also considered the epicenter of the city's gay community. Moving downtown provided me with a new sense of autonomy and status. From its breathtaking monuments and eclectic neighborhoods to its diverse population, everything about DC was sophisti-cated—the crowded streets, exotic strangers, and quaint cafés. Graduating from relationship hopping, I was now dating several men simultaneously. Here I was, living life in the fast lane in one of the most elite and powerful cities in the world, staunchly pro-choice and fully liberated.

Working as a secretary for a swanky law firm totally eclipsed from being employed as a clerk for the government. There were beautiful offices, twice-a-year bonus checks, and a myriad of new people to get to know. Male lawyers wore Brooks Brother's suits, starched shirts, and paisley neckties. Women were wear-ing bow blouses and earth-tone polyester pant-suits. But the biggest trend in female fashion during this time was shoulder pads and a severe drop to the waist to create the "power look." Maybe women's lib had some effect on this style as women were having more influence in the workplace.

My new coworkers were diverse, cool, and hip. They ranged in age from twenty-five to sixty. At nineteen, I was the baby of the bunch. Quite a few were single, successful women whom I instantly wanted to emulate. So when Rosie, my officemate, invited me out after work for drinks I enthusiastically accepted. She knew of a club called Tiffany's that offered low-priced drinks and dancing during happy hour. Dancing during happy hour! I loved the idea. And to top it off, it featured rhythm and blues.

Growing up so close to the city gave me an uncommon awareness of backgrounds and cultures. This unity within diversity allowed for some deeply rooted prejudices to be swept aside. Through the years I had many black friends, even when it wasn't cool, when it was still taboo on both sides. I fell in love with many attributes of the black culture. There was a close-ness of family that I really admired. My black friends would visit their grandmothers, aunts, or uncles every other day. Every chance possible, the whole family would gather for a meal. This wasn't just some ordinary, run of the mill meal—it was soul food. Fried chicken, mac 'n' cheese, collards, and cornbread. Even now, my mouth waters just thinking about it. Although my family had many family dinners with great food, I always felt envious of my black friends' gatherings, since my grandparents lived hundreds of miles away and we only visited a few times a year.

This was the era when most of us still felt bulletproof.

One of the things that had the most significant and profound effect on my life was the introduction to rhythm and blues—soul music. I loved the beat, the words, and the entire vibe. Nothing held back. That was me! We would groove to the Chi-Lites, Earth, Wind & Fire, Gladys Knight & The Pips, Al Green, and the Al Green. When Bobby Womack would start to sing "If You Think You're Lonely Now" the hair on my arms would stand up and I would be transported into another world—one of love, joy, and unity. These relationships gave me the ability to see beyond color into people's hearts.

For many in this era, the ultimate champion was the person who was narcissistic. Success was measured by how much money a person made and what kind of toys he or she owned. I always seemed to attract men who had the "hero" persona: they were rich, handsome, fence-sitters, never willing to commit to a relationship. This type of man intrigued me; I thought they could fulfill in me that which I felt was missing. This was what attracted me to Markus: he was tall, dark, and totally captivating. We drank, danced, and exchanged numbers. I literally got tremors when he drove away in his silver Mercedes. I didn't know quite what to make of him, but I wanted to know more.

We began to date occasionally. He was very secretive, and I was very naïve. I was always one step ahead with the guys I was

dating; I set the rules and boundaries. Never had I met anyone who dished it out the same way I could. When our paths
crossed it was exciting and provocative; but when they didn't
I continued to live a very liberated life style—dating multiple
men simultaneously and sleeping with each of them. Societal
emphases on virginity and marriage were being replaced by
sexual freedom and singleness, and I was going to experience
it all.

Sex and sexuality was an acceptable topic to discuss during
the 1980s; but unlike today, sexually transmitted diseases were
not. For young singles, free sex was not only unobjectionable, it
was encouraged. Although the herpes virus began to threaten
society in the mid-1970s and syphilis and gonorrhea were on
the rise, prevention was not a talking point. Condoms were
used to prevent pregnancy, and the term *safe sex* hadn't yet come
on the scene. This was the era when most of us still felt bulletproof. I certainly did. I'd heard the rumors that you could catch
gonorrhea from a toilet seat or at the swimming pool; but I
knew when I was diagnosed, that I got it from neither.

I was drinking, smoking pot, snorting cocaine, and having
a lot of casual sex. However, the possibility of contracting a
venereal disease never occurred to me. Feeling the pain that
I thought was a bladder infection, I headed off to the doctor.
Although I was a bit shocked when I was diagnosed with gonorrhea, so affectionately referred to as VD, I lied when they
asked about my partner referral. When the doctor told me I
needed to contact my sexual partner(s) and let him/them know
I was infected, I said of course I would but never contacted a
soul. Being concerned basically with only myself, I did what I
had to do to get through life.

We can all find a way to cope. I would mentally put all
my uncomfortable decisions, like abortion and addiction, in a
box and hide them away. This blocked any negative feelings

I had in relation to difficult situations, but it also blocked helpful information from getting through. Unknowingly, I was making contributions to the hardening of my heart—like Bernie had done and Kathy would do with their own hearts.

Bernie didn't see how his desire to help women, which somehow became legalizing abortion on demand, would cause himself lifelong emotional and physical pain and suffering. As for Kathy, because of her abuse, her innocence and vulnerability were stolen—she put up a fortress of protection. She was taught that she could not be wrong; it would be too damaging to her well-being. My answer to my current dilemma was to take the penicillin and stay away from all the guys with whom I had had sexual relations the prior month. This opened the floodgate for new experiences, with new partners, which created another problem: I became pregnant again. If an occasional penicillin prescription was the price I had to pay to continue my open lifestyle, then it would be paid. VD was one thing; pregnancy was much more inconvenient and expensive to abort.

Since I had multiple sex partners, I really had no idea who, other than me, was responsible for this unfortunate circumstance. What I was sure of was that I would terminate the pregnancy. Because of Dr. Vuitch's rudeness and all-around rough bedside manner during my last procedure, I didn't want to return to the Laurel Clinic. Doing some research, I located a clinic named Planned Parenthood on 16th Street just a few blocks from the White House. When I called, they were very professional and answered all my questions completely. When they asked how far along I was, I answered "ten or eleven weeks." They encouraged me to make my appointment as soon as possible because after twelve weeks the price would go up. My response was to ask for their next opening.

With my appointment set for the end of that week, I had some thinking to do. Which of my recent partners could and would come up with the $150? After two calls, my knight in shining armor surfaced, probably because he didn't want his wife to find out he was sleeping around.

Living at DuPont Circle, the clinic was a three-dollar cab ride away. Arriving at Planned Parenthood that morning, I paid cash at the front desk and sat in a small, crowded waiting room. The procedure was similar to my previous abortion; however, the pain was not as intense, and it seemed quicker. Also, this doctor didn't raise his voice, in fact he never said a word or even made eye contact. After the abortion I was taken to a room with several cots and was given orange juice and crackers. I was in and out of the door in no time at all. No time for questions, answers, or reflection. Knowing what to expect, I took a cab home, got a six pack of beer from the deli on the corner, rolled a joint, and hunkered down for a night of solitude with my TV. This abortion stuff was physically painful and dreadfully expensive—$150 in 1978 being about like $850 in 2016—but I was at liberty to enter into my future without the unwanted responsibility of a child. I believed the liberated mantra of the day: *It is my body, and I have the right to choose what I do with it.*

> I was making contributions to the hardening of my heart.

Meanwhile, my career at the law firm was going well and afforded me the ability to live a double life—party at night and show up hungover frequently. My "drinking and drugging" was on the rise, especially my cocaine use. But I was young and able to bounce back quickly; by noon I was usually back on track. Although already receiving pay increases, I seized every occasion to earn the extra bucks that allowed me to live the lifestyle I craved. Having the opportunity to work as much overtime as I liked, I began picking up hours over weekends. Most of the time I was the only person in the office working, which

provided me with much flexibility. This is when I began to fal-
sify my time sheets.

Living so close to the office, I would pop in and out on
Saturday or Sunday long enough to turn on my electric type-
writer, make a pot of coffee, and make it obvious that someone
had been there. Because my pop-ins were
synchronized, I could cover my tracks if
anyone showed up, or so I thought. Being
cocky, I believed I would never get caught.
One Saturday it all came to an abrupt end
when the managing partner of the firm
showed up and worked for most of the
day. He was there, and I wasn't—even though I said I was. It
was messy, and I was exposed. I was fired the next Monday
morning on the spot.

> My life was on the
> upward path—
> my bank account
> said so.

One would think this would have been a devastating blow
and an ego-deflating learning experience. Oh no, not for me.
Justification kicked in, as well as unemployment benefits. This
gave me some breathing room and time to find out what I
really wanted to do with my life. Being a freethinker and a
social butterfly, I thought that surely there was a career that
would utilize these talents. Deciding to go back to school to
train for a different career, I enrolled at Bartenders Academy.
Graduating with flying colors, I landed a job at the infamous
Gangplank restaurant down at the Wharf.

The three-martini lunch was at its height during the early
'80s, and the restaurant was famous for great seafood and an
outstanding view of the harbor. Customers with high-ranking
government positions and other sleek Capitol Hill types fre-
quented the place daily. The restaurant was also smack in the
middle of the Washington DC Marina, a place that boasted its
own procession of elite clientele. The money I was making far

outweighed any forged time sheet mess I left behind. My life was on the upward path—my bank account said so.

There I was, brazenly living life on the edge, breaking out of all the contemporary molds, wearing nice clothes, fine perfume, and living in a fancy apartment. According to *Cosmopolitan* and *Ms.* magazines, I had it all. So if I did, why was I feeling desperately empty and unfulfilled? I was young, attractive, making money, living free of commitment or consequence—I had the world by the tail, nowhere to go but up. But the sizzle was gone. I found myself growing bored. Except, that is, when it came to Markus. Although martini lunches were chic, and dating around was acceptable, interracial relationships were not. I wanted people to see me with Markus; I liked the notoriety and the uniqueness of our union. It was unconventional. However, in my quest for excitement, I underestimated two very powerful things: my affection for Markus and my craving for cocaine. Knowing both were taboo, I desired them more, striving for the forbidden. The more society said "you shouldn't," the more I said "I shall." After all, I was born and bred during a time of change and rebellion. The idealism generated by the women's revolution and the civil rights movement helped inspire my opposition to tradition, allowing me to fight for my own beliefs. *Isn't that what America is all about,* I thought, *standing up for what we believe, fighting for our own convictions?*

Although Markus and I were both looking for something, for someone, the more I coveted my relationship with him, the more aloof he became. Even though I was attached to Markus, I wasn't going to take a back seat to anyone. After a run-in with one of his other "babes" and facing the realization that I wasn't the only one, I made an executive decision to relocate and get out of town so he could experience life without me: the first of my geographic "cures."

I moved to Ocean City, Maryland, in the late spring of 1981, and lived in my parents' beach house. In no time, the Sheraton Pool Bar was mine. I had created a new relational web and started hanging out at the oceanside hotspots. The Beach Club was truly where it was at: live music every night, lots of booze, and handsome men. I would work all day, grab something to eat, buy a new outfit for the night, and zip home. My nap would refresh me for my nighttime ritual, and then I was off. My new friends were well connected in the "after-hours" community, and before long I had cultivated my own connections to drugs. So in addition to a meal and a new outfit, most days also included a stop by the coke man's pad.

Many nights I was out until the sun came up, and on occasion I would go from the party where I crashed to pull my shift at the Sheraton. Though I had many different relationships, there was still an aching in my heart for Markus. He did just enough to keep it going, like showing up at the pool bar one day, out of the blue, and renting a suite in the hotel. He had an entire evening planned to woo me back, and it worked. I just couldn't shake him. *It must be love, true love*, I thought. This all worked great as long as I was at the beach and he was in Hyattsville, Maryland—one hundred and seventy miles away.

By the end of the summer a group of people who were in a popular band, Second Coming, decided to open a night-club in Greenbelt, Maryland. This was about twenty miles from my childhood home and, more importantly, only twenty miles from Hyattsville. Everyone who was anyone was working at the club, so I thought I probably wouldn't have a chance for a spot. Once again, the chips fell in my favor and I was in. I moved in with my parents again until I could get my own place.

The club took its name from its founders, Second Coming, and it was the most awesome night spot in the area. Nightclubs with live bands or DJs were all the rage, and the club was jumping from lunchtime, through happy hour, and until the wee hours of the morning. On good days we would make about $150–175 during a six-to-seven-hour shift. Many of our regular customers were also "holding"—in possession of a vial with a teeny, tiny spoon, or a bullet top filled with that glorious white powder. Everyone had it, from top execs to policemen to school teachers. Everyone had a different story and a unique desire to escape life. In those days, at least in most bars or clubs, it was a rarity if you weren't into cocaine.

Immediately I picked up where I left off with Markus, but he continued to remain aloof. He never wanted to give me or my friends the impression that we were a couple. Our usual routine was that we saw each other at his house after I got off work at 2:00 or 3:00 a.m. This didn't leave much time for socializing, just a late-night booty call.

> Everyone had a different story and a unique desire to escape life.

There were those occasional nights I went home, to my parents' house, when I needed to catch up on my sleep, and I often joined my parents' nightly tradition of watching the eleven o'clock news. So I can recall one particular night's newscast with complete clarity: the headline, "Abortionist Dr. Milan Vuitch Exposed" flashed across the TV screen.

My heart jumped into my throat! I sat there in astonishment, unable to even react. Channel 9 News had done an investigative report on the Laurel Clinic and on Vuitch. "The investigation found that Vuitch's practice had been cited for a multitude of violations, such as in 1980, for dirty instruments and lab specimens being refrigerated with food; in 1981, for Vuitch's having taking patients to his home overnight and having expired drugs; in 1982, for unlicensed drug distribution, mixing dirty and clean surgical instruments, and sending a patient home although she was passing red urine and had a catheter still inside her body; in 1983, for having anesthetic drugs "not freshly prepared and yellowish in color." The investigator also noted that despite these violations, the city kept renewing the clinic's license until 1982, after which Vuitch just operated without one."[1]

This was the same man who had performed my first abortion, the man who was supposedly skilled and well experienced! My mind raced, and I felt extremely uneasy. I wondered if my parents thought I was acting weird. I couldn't say anything to anyone—there was no one who would understand. What if I had been one of his victims? It just took me a few more years to understand the effects of what I had done—and of what he had done to me—and I came to realize that I had indeed been one of his victims.

I had trouble sleeping that night, feeling really uneasy about what I had seen on the news, so I drank myself into oblivion. I got up the next morning, nursing a fierce headache and pushing any residual effects from the news report as far out of my mind as possible. I got ready to face another day. A day that would include my main man—Markus.

Markus was unlike anyone I had ever met. He was handsome, rich, and eccentric; and I wanted everyone to meet him. After a few months of my non-stop "Markus talk" to coworkers, he finally showed up one night—waltzed in wearing his cowboy hat and custom-made suit. He was met with mixed responses. Some people saw him for what he was, an arrogant man who was full of himself. Others, the ones whose opinions I preferred, found him to be exceptionally charming. Until this time Markus had not been a habitual cocaine user, but things began to change rapidly.

Even though I had been at the beach living it up, I stayed in contact with my friend Courtney. She was still married to Johnny and was now a mom, but every once in a while we would get together and make something happen in a big way—go all out! One such night, we wanted to cop some coke. I called Markus, and he said he had some and would meet us at the New Carrollton Metro parking lot. We drove the thirty-mile trip from Edgewater, Maryland, and waited for over an hour. No show. As soon as we got back to Courtney's house in that pre-cell phone era, I called him, seething. He again promised to meet me. Again we made the trip. Again he was a no show. Later that night, I went by his house and found out why he hadn't shown up. He had been free-basing cocaine.

As I mentioned earlier, smoking cocaine hits your nervous system so fast that it literally makes you immobile. But the high is so short lived, lasting no more than twenty minutes, that you continually crave your next hit. Oftentimes you won't leave your source or the place where you are getting high due to this vicious cycle of demand.

I had tried free-basing once, months before at a party, but never really got much out of it, until now. One hit and I was hooked. The entire process from acquiring the exquisite white powder, to breaking it down in the cooking process, to cleaning the screens, finding a lighter, and inhaling the thick, fragrant smoke was the adventure I had been searching for. My emotional, physical, and mental desires were fulfilled, if only for ten intense, euphoric minutes. There was nothing or no one who could offer me fulfillment like the rock and the pipe. There was no long engagement or "getting to know one another" period; I fell hopelessly into a full-blown, all-encompassing, outrageous, overwhelming, mesmerizing affair. From the first moment, I was truly faithful, always seeking, yearning, and desiring more of my newfound love. I was willing to do anything for it; truly, I would have died for it. The only question now was how I could mesh this magnificent relationship, this all-encompassing love, into my everyday life. No one would understand, but it was crucial that I formulate my life to fit into my covenant with cocaine. Finally, I had uncovered the remedy to satisfy my soul.

Coco Channel had nothing on me—I was fabulous, all right!

12

KATHY

New Lease on Life

"Perfectionism is a self-destructive and addictive belief system
that fuels this primary thought: If I look perfect, and do
everything perfectly, I can avoid or minimize the
painful feelings of shame, judgment, and blame."

~BRENÉ BROWN

After that freeing encounter with God on the lakeshore, an
enormous weight lifted. I navigated four years at a major university in Seattle, the city I had been afraid to even visit for the
King Tut exhibit in high school. And I loved it. Busier than
ever on and off campus, I joined a college ministry group and
pursued spiritual development with—well, with religious fervor! I felt like God had given me a new lease on life, and I
wanted to be sure I was doing the "right" things to keep it that
way. Not that gratitude was my main motivation. I had adopted
a philosophy that said if I could master the right behavior such
as making good grades, following a moral code, or helping others, then my life would turn out all right. What I didn't realize was that this quid pro quo mentality completely misses the
heart of unconditional love. In my head I knew spirituality was

supposed to be about relationship, not a contract with God. So I gave lip service to believing He is good, to believing God didn't owe me anything. But I had no idea I was actually attempting to manipulate my Creator.

At the end of each spring semester, just when I'd had all the studying and campus life I could handle, I'd pack my bags and head to that same Colorado Rocky Mountain dude ranch I'd loved as a child, only this time as part of the summer staff. Immersed in the breathtaking scenery, for three months every summer I roamed the trails on horseback, leading an entourage of vacationing kids behind me. Under a black, unpolluted sky draped with a blanket of stars, evenings were spent with young faces around a campfire, bumping along on a hayride, or swing dancing with the guests and staff to a live country band. Those summer months were incredible.

Making a great experience even better, several times each summer my brother, Steve, would make his way to the ranch to visit me. Together we'd hike the mountains we both loved. It meant a lot to me that he'd take off work and drive the distance just to be with me. Time had transformed our friendship as we each grew out of our teenage extremes. Unlike anyone I was really close to, he impressed and intimidated me at the same time. Steve had become a profoundly compassionate and kind man. He was a deep thinker, passionate about injustice and the disenfranchised, and didn't toe the conservative line so common in my circles. I felt smarter just being around him.

Lingering on a mountainside overlooking miles of snowy peaks and valleys of aspen and pine trees, our long conversations would cover a wide range of topics. We debated political issues and talked about music we loved. We laughed at my latest adventure with kids on trail rides or his climbing through the rafters to get backstage and meet band members at a rock concert. We opened up about our individual struggles and tried to make sense of our religious training in light of the world we encountered. Steve wrestled with legitimate questions, and we would talk through his conflicted feelings about the Christian God he'd been raised with. He invested genuine effort in searching out answers to his spiritual questions. "I'm finding my way back to God," he reassured me. "I just don't think it's going to look like what I grew up with."

> Time had transformed our friendship as we each grew out of our teenage extremes.

I was broadening my horizons, too, so I had some understanding but didn't know how to really process the depth of his angst. I was fixated on finding the right actions to give me inner peace; and I was still drawing my sense of self from the small circle I hung around, from my accomplishments, and from my family's identity. Steve, on the other hand, far from identifying with us, explored a much bigger and darker world on his own. Our differences bothered me a little—wouldn't it be better if we all saw things the same way? But those thoughts were few and far between while I led a busy life at the ranch and at school.

My senior year of college, while I remained in Seattle, my family moved back to our hometown in Colorado, and I flew home for the Christmas break. In the midst of last-minute shopping and catching up with family, I was invited to a surprise birthday party for a friend. When I walked into the room on the night of the party, I was the one who was surprised. The birthday boy, someone I'd known since the eighth grade, was all of a sudden "Mr. Tall, Dark, and Handsome" and looking really good to me! This kind of blew my mind because Dave and I had hung out only three months earlier, and for sure no fireworks were going off then. They say timing is everything!

We spent time together every day over the holidays. How he treated me made quite an impression. Protective but not possessive, he made me feel both valued and at ease. He opened doors, and he opened his heart. He was well dressed, and I liked how he carried himself with confidence. He treated his mom with gentleness and respect. He was direct but not demanding in letting me know his intentions toward me. He was smart, witty, and he made laugh.

We dated long distance through my last semester of college, and after graduation I moved back home to Colorado. Six months after that surprise birthday, over a romantic dinner in a penthouse restaurant, a waiter brought me a glass of champagne with a diamond ring in it and Dave was down on one knee asking me to marry him. That same year on a frozen white day in December, we were married in a setting filled with windows looking out on snow-laden pine trees. Walking down the aisle, I was never surer of any decision in my life. That day I felt like the luckiest girl in the world.

But reality has a way of settling back in, and it didn't take long for some of my familiar struggles to resurface. Although I had graduated with a degree in nutrition, I didn't have a career and had frequent doubts about my purpose. Wasn't I supposed to do something monumental with my life? Make my mark? Coming from a strongly academic background and a family full of leaders, I slipped back into comparison mode. We lived in the same town with our extended families, and we were surrounded by highly intelligent people. I was terribly insecure and convinced that I needed to be smart to be valued. I definitely didn't feel smart around these folks.

A big part of our culture was gathering together for meals and game nights. Trivial Pursuit had just made its debut and was the game of choice when we hung out with friends or my family. On multiple occasions, I was in tears on the drive back to our townhouse, feeling stupid and humiliated. Especially after an evening with Steve—now married—and his wife and my folks. Someone would pull a card with a ridiculously obscure question, and I'd laugh to myself thinking, *Good grief! No one could possibly know that!* Then, sure enough, after a few moments of pondering, one of them would come up with the answer, and my self-esteem would go down the toilet. Dave would try to reassure me on the way home. "Sweetie, there's a reason it's called 'Trivial Pursuit'—it's TRIVIAL!" But it wasn't trivial to me. It was a sure sign in my mind that I was stupid.

In addition to feelings of ignorance and worthlessness, ever present was the ongoing problem of being startled awake with the intense nightmares. I had given my husband fair warning that I would probably wake up screaming a couple of nights a week—and I did, shocking him out of sleep along with me. In the daylight, however, I was fearless. No more fears of abandonment. No panic attacks. Since that day by the lake, I think I instinctively knew that to feel too much was dangerous—it could lead to out-of-control terror. The only emotions I really found acceptable were feeling happy or feeling inadequate and resolving to try harder. I rarely cried except at the movies or when I felt lonely or ashamed.

I had great trouble empathizing deeply with anyone. I felt bad for you, but I couldn't bring myself to cry with you. Don't get me wrong, I wasn't coldhearted, I just didn't know how to access those emotions. William Paul Young, author of *The Shack*, put it this way: "You can't pick which emotions to shut down. It's an all or nothing process."[1]

I dedicated a lot of energy to "doing everything right." Of course, what's really senseless about this approach to life is this: How do you figure out what is right? Everyone has a different opinion. Just try googling any parenting technique and you'll get ten different answers, strongly opinionated, to the same question. Attempting to get all your ducks in a row so that your life will be successful is like trying to hit a moving target. Not that I ever consciously thought this way—it was a life motto I couldn't put into words. But I had a desperate need to see myself as doing well and have others see me that way too. Pairing my perfectionism with an imagined religious ideal, I wound up entrenched in a cycle of perfectionism and comparison. A sense of well-being only settled in me if my outside circumstances lined up with my ideal. I was back to trying to control all the externals to grab onto some fleeting internal peace.

> I had a desperate need to see myself as doing well and have others see me that way too.

Seven years into our marriage, two little sons had been added to our family. I never knew how much joy I could actually feel before these precious gifts came into my life! I was gradually beginning to feel a broader range of emotions. Deeper love, more laughter—and greater anxiety. Now, with a family at stake, I became even more invested in pursuing "excellence." I just had to get this right. I put a whole lot of things in the "must have" category. Top-notch nutrition in our home, naturally, and the best activities and religious training for our preschool boys. Creating the perfect house (always clean, of course), saying yes to anyone who asked for my help (a complete lack of boundaries), and reading books on how to make sure I was pleasing God. And I especially wanted my husband to behave in a way that showed me, and everyone else, he wasn't just a great guy, he was Mr. Super Spiritual. Was that too much to ask?

I was obsessing over all of this while my ongoing nightmares kept me perpetually sleep deprived. And I was failing. Everyone was failing. My husband simply refused to play some exaggerated religious role. Stubbornly, he was determined to just be—of all things—himself! He was content to quietly live out his spirituality, loving his wife and being a good dad to his sons.

It never occurred to me to question the absurdity of my standards. I just redoubled my efforts. I had to get it "right." Everyone else seemed to be doing better than I was. This mental obsession with comparison choked much of the life out of pursuits that ignited my passion. Songwriting and performing were deep loves of mine, but from my view someone else was always a more talented musician. I thrived with education, but someone else was always more well-informed, smarter than I was. Family and home were precious to me, but I just couldn't compete as a decorator. Not only did this mindset stir up feelings of low self-worth, but it unleashed the ugly green-eyed monster of jealousy. Jealousy, that subtle thief, steals the dignity of others and robs us of our value. I just couldn't get it all together. My house was never totally decluttered. And you guessed it, my self-esteem would go right back down the toilet. I felt "less than" and frustrated.

Steve and I continued with our occasional hang-out times. He'd drop by my house or I'd visit his, and we'd linger for an hour catching up. He would tell me about the latest NPR report, a documentary I needed to see, or show me music that had yet to hit the mainstream. I'd catch him up on Dave and the boys, music I was writing, and the latest issues I was thinking through. I loved talking with him one on one.

And he was Johnny-on-the-spot for me in emergencies when my husband was out of town on business. Like the time when I was eight months pregnant with our first son and a raccoon got stuck in our trash can. He came right over, balanced on the fence to topple the trash can, and swung the gate open to set the not-so-little critter free. But these visits with him weren't nearly as frequent as the time the rest of the extended family spent together. We were big on family gatherings and outings; and although Steve and his wife jumped in on some of them, he kept more to himself. It began to occur to me that we were all over here playing board games while my brother was out living a totally different life.

From time to time he'd confide in me that he still struggled with substance abuse, which was something I couldn't even begin to relate to at the time. It was such a contrast to what I knew about his life. He was extremely generous, deeply compassionate, and always ready to help—especially the elderly and the poor. His actions were marked by genuine humility. He once saved a family from a house fire and disappeared before they were able to thank him or even catch his name!

It was hard for me to comprehend his demons, so different from mine. That we both struggled trying to get on the right track bothered me. I worried about him and obsessed about me. In the back of my mind I kept thinking, *Just give it time. It will get better.*

One sunny morning in April after leading an aerobics class, I hurried through our front door to pick up a ringing phone. Dressed in workout clothes, with a baby on my hip and a toddler at my side, I heard my parents' voices on the other end of the line. Nothing could have prepared me for what I heard next.

"Honey, we have some terrible news. Steve has been murdered."

13

BERNIE

A Change of Mind

"It was then that I began
the painful process of changing my mind."

~Dr. Bernard Nathanson

Defining moments are significant events or decisions that alter the course of a life. Something shifts. We either move closer to or further away from discovering our true purpose in life. In that single evening, sitting next to Lawrence Lader at that pivotal dinner party, the course of Bernie's life shifted. Swept up in the momentum of cofounding NARAL, he was thrust full speed into forcing massive change in abortion laws. Just six years later, an encounter with an unborn child via ultrasound drastically altered the trajectory of his life once again. The first path Bernie chose was motivated by a determination to fix a societal problem—an external focus. The second decision, after seeing the humanity of the unborn, revealed an internal path on which Bernie "began the painful process of changing [his] mind."[1]

Seeing the unborn child through the ultrasound sparked a frightening and mesmerizing awakening in his soul. There in front of him he saw a beating heart, tiny hands and feet in motion, a living being serenely cradled. In that moment, after years of championing the expectant mother, he discovered with alarming clarity that he had, in fact, *another patient in the room!* "For the first time as a physician, I began to understand that more was involved in an abortion than merely suctioning out a mass of cells, a few grams of tissue. I began to be aware that there was something here which had a moral destiny to it which commanded respect."[2]

During the middle-to-late 1970s, he found himself burning with a disturbing moral conflict. In a not uncommon practice, he was delivering babies at twenty-three weeks of life and desperately trying to save them on one floor of the hospital while aborting babies at the same gestational age just one floor below. Which life had more value? To Bernie, it had formerly been all about a woman's situation. Suddenly, this was about a life, not a "situation." He began to wonder, *Why does it matter where the baby resides?* It was apparent to him now that the baby wasn't just a circumstance but an actual human being.

Bernie's perspective didn't transform overnight. No blinding light and voice out of the heavens for this avowed atheist. But he was willing to consider the possibility he had been wrong. How much do we miss by refusing to loosen our death grip on our precious assumptions? Lisa was convinced that drugs and alcohol were the solution to her problems even though they were destroying every relationship in her life and assassinating her own identity. Kathy was convinced that perfection and performance would save her. They were each in a vicious cycle, just like Bernie.

Armed with his newfound information, Bernie began to reevaluate his perspective carefully, meticulously—and privately. Abortion law reform had released a tsunami of demand in New York City and across the nation. Implementing the vast changes had left Bernie wrung out and disillusioned. All he had wanted was to provide safe abortions for those in desperate need, but it was spinning out of control. Abortion was now legalized up to the twenty-fourth week of pregnancy in New York. Up to this time this had seemed to Bernie like a reasonable, humane service for women. But the language of the ruling in *Roe v. Wade* in 1973 was so vague it actually lifted all restrictions not only in New York, but across the country. Incredibly, physicians could legally perform abortions into the ninth month of pregnancy just as long as the woman had not felt the first pang of labor! Even with recent laws enacted, this is still possible today! This was not at all what the young revolutionary doctor had envisioned during his residency.

> Putting his ego aside, he was fearless and thorough in examining all aspects of abortion.

He stayed on as a board member of NARAL, but he lost all enthusiasm for the cause and became less and less involved. During their 1972 convention, the last he ever attended, he robotically presented his report on abortion clinic safety. He slipped out quietly after his speech. In his own words, "I felt a stranger in their midst, as if I had somehow bloodied myself in the cause, and they were still clean and dry."[3]

Bernie picked a confidant with whom to reason through his growing doubts. They spent long hours sorting through the complex moral dilemma he faced. Putting his ego aside, he was fearless and thorough in examining all aspects of abortion.

As a result of these conversations, in 1974, the article "Deeper into Abortion" appeared in the *New England Journal of Medicine*. In it Nathanson expressed his growing doubts and fears about presiding over what he estimated to be 75,000 deaths.[4] Bernie now declared that *the human fetus is life*. "We must courageously face the fact—finally—that human life of a special order is being taken. And since the vast majority of pregnancies are carried successfully to term, abortion must be seen as the interruption of a process that would otherwise have produced a citizen of the world. Denial of this reality is the crassest kind of moral evasiveness."[5]

This statement provoked an outcry within the medical community. No physician had dared to publically question the morality of his fellow colleagues. After all, they did have a god complex. That single article received the largest response of any article before or since published in the *New England Journal of Medicine*. He was completely unprepared for that reaction. Unlike before, when he had manipulated the media, now Dr. Nathanson became an instant abortion celebrity, highlighted across the nation in the press and interviewed on multiple radio and TV stations. He was inundated with sacks of mail, phone calls, and even threats against his life and his family. Clearly, he had hit a nerve. Even though he continued to toe the NARAL line of total abortion on request, his former cohorts vilified him. They demanded unswerving loyalty, no questions asked.[6] And Nathanson was asking questions! He found himself in the center of a raging debate and had become an outcast.

That didn't stop him. He shifted his focus, pouring his energy into fetology, the study of the pre-born. The growing mountains of evidence revealing the humanity of the fetus overwhelmed his senses. The Hippocratic Oath to "do no harm" served as his mantra during his research. The more Bernie's research intersected with the tiny lives of the unborn, the greater his passion grew to protect them. He agonized as research discovered the fetus feels pain as early as seven weeks of gestation and feels the same intensity of pain by the twentieth week that an adult does. With sickening alarm, he recalculated that he had presided over seventy-five thousand abortions, five thousand by his own hands, including one of his own children. By the end of the 1970s, he had concluded with absolute certainty that the fetus is a human life and abortion is murder.

Wasting no time, Bernie did an about-face. With his new-found convictions firmly in place, Dr. Nathanson jumped into the deep end of the pro-life movement, never looking back. Bernie concluded that "there was no reason for an abortion at any time. This person in the womb is a living human being and we could not continue to wage war against the most defenseless of human beings."[7] Make no mistake, this was not a religious or emotional conversion. For Dr. Bernard Nathanson, it was a purely scientific conclusion. He became a sought-after speaker and attended many pro-life vigils. All the while he kept his scientific mind disengaged from the spiritual motivations of the majority of his new comrades. Evidence and logic were what mattered. Dr. Nathanson threw himself into writing a factual, intellectual argument against abortion and published his book *Aborting America* in 1979. At that time, a higher moral authority didn't merely fail to move him, it didn't even exist in his mind. But all that was about to change.

During an encounter several years later, his perspective was once again drastically altered. After speaking to a pro-life state convention, he approached a woman he'd come to admire for her calm and intellectual approach to complex questions. When it came to abortion, this level-headed woman became intense and angry. Bernie asked her why. She stared back at him, shocked at his lack of comprehension.

Her reply went something like this, "Doctor, what if you heard screams coming from an exam room and walked in on a mother beating her six-week-old infant with a blunt instrument? Seeing blood everywhere, and the baby grotesquely deformed and unrecognizable, would you try to stop it? But what if you were told it was legal? Not only that but it was in the best interest of the infant and the mother? And what if you encountered this day in and day out for ten years and were powerless to stop it? You'd get pretty heated up too!"

With that, something clicked inside. Bernie's heart came alive, engaged, never to lose its passion again. After publishing *Aborting America*, he immediately began a second book, this time writing more from anger, and as a result published *The Abortion Papers* in 1983.

The weight of the obliteration of these tiny, helpless citizens began to take its toll.

Having learned the powerful effect of the media through engineering the pro-abortion campaign, Dr. Nathanson concocted another approach. Bernie called on a friend for a favor. He asked an abortionist colleague to film an ultrasound during an actual abortion. The mother gave her consent, and the doctor happily obliged. The resulting video shook Bernie, his colleague, and the expectant mother to the core. When they sat down to edit the film, the abortionist was so disturbed by what he saw he was forced to leave the room several times to regain his composure. He was devastated by what he had done with his own hands. He never performed another abortion. The poor mother was so deeply affected that she never spoke of it again or sought another abortion.

What they filmed graphically shows the serene fetus suddenly scramble away from the instruments that were searching to latch onto it. The tiny heart started to beat wildly out of control. The final act of this little life was to let out a silent scream as it helplessly succumbed to execution.

With this, Bernie had all the evidence he needed. He was confronted by the enormity of the evil he had been perpetrating. Taking decisive action, in 1984 he produced the film, calling it *The Silent Scream*. It aired five times on national television and was widely distributed on college campuses. President Reagan privately viewed the documentary and was so deeply grieved he stated, "It's been said that if every member of Congress could see that film, they would move quickly to end the tragedy of abortion, and I pray that they will."[8]

Bernie didn't know that thirty-one years later we would be in a similar situation: an outcry for all members of Congress to watch the videos exposing Planned Parenthood for selling aborted baby parts for profit. Interestingly, he did speak prophetically about the harvesting of baby parts in his book *The Hand of God: A Journey from Death to Life by the Abortion Doctor Who Changed His Mind*.[9]

Not only was Dr. Nathanson deeply disturbed by the suffering he witnessed and recorded in the *Silent Scream*, he was especially troubled by the brutality of harvesting human brain tissue. He wrote, "Pregnant women, 13–18 weeks, are placed on an operating table, the cervix is dilated and the bag of water is broken, the fetal head is guided into position just above the open cervix. The fetal skull is drilled open and a suction device is placed into the brain. The brain tissue is then suctioned out and placed immediately on ice to preserve its viability. The fetus is *then* aborted."[10] Keep in mind that this little body experiences excruciating pain.

Critics claimed that the ultrasound film was a fake. Incensed, Bernie sent the film to the inventor of the ultrasound to authenticate it, which he did with absolute certainty. Bernie didn't stop there; he did one better. He filmed a late-term abortion using an actual camera inside the womb. The film begins with a compelling introduction by Charlton Heston and includes heart-wrenching testimonials of post-abortive women. He released the film *Eclipse of Reason* in 1987.

In spite of Bernie's tireless efforts, abortion on demand gained momentum like a runaway train. The weight of the obliteration of these tiny, helpless citizens began to take its toll. The intellectually ethical doctor with an ever-growing passion fell headlong into a season of torment. Night after night he was awakened at 3:00 a.m., terrorized by his contribution to the monstrosity of abortion. He referred to himself as a mass murderer. He chillingly describes his torment in *The Abortion Papers:* "I know every facet of abortion. I helped nurture the creature in its infancy by feeding it great draughts of blood and money; I guided it through its adolescence as it grew fecklessly out of control."[11] With this unforgivable burden pressing on his soul, Bernie contemplated suicide almost nightly. Night after night he would talk himself out of it, pitifully hoping to undo the damage he had incited. However, it was in the darkness of those agonizingly long nights that the unsuspecting doctor would encounter yet another defining moment—one that would change him forever.

14

LISA

Geographic Cure

"I think many people can relate
to that excruciating pain of love gone wrong.
I'd rather have a broken arm than a broken heart."

~CHRISTIE BRINKLEY

Everything in my life was pursued in accordance with my feelings and emotions. Moment by moment I surveyed what I wanted. Prevalent were the two loves in my life—cocaine and Markus—in that order.

The Second Coming nightclub provided a steady job and flow of money. Anxious to move out of my parents' house, I put the word out that I was looking for a place to live. So when Roger, one of my regular happy hour customers, told me he was looking for a roommate I was ecstatic. He was a well-known coke dealer and always had great parties.

But all good things come to an end, and eventually Second Coming closed its doors. One of my former happy-hour regulars was opening a new club in the heart of DC. It was to be called The Board Room—glamorous and alluring, with all the ambience of a Las Vegas social establishment.

Working at the pool bar and in the nightclub scene, I had grown used to unconventional clothing. In fact, the more provocative the attire, the better I liked it. But in this job, the apparel wasn't the only unique thing; it was the opportunity. I wasn't being offered a bartending position, but that of a show-girl/waitress. The job included dancing on the tables in the cocktail lounge. Although I wasn't the prudish type, this idea was a bit uncomfortable for me. Still, I wasn't the "take some time and ponder" type: if it feels good, do it! I pushed away any reservation and hesitation that could hinder this financial opportunity and took the job. Remember, I was woman—and yes, you could hear me roar! I loved the attention. For weeks we were fitted for costumes, given dance lessons, and trotted out in rehearsals until the week of the opening, when, as they say, the bottom fell out. The Board Room never opened because they could not obtain the operating permit.

As uncomfortable as it had been for me to take this job, it was easy for it to become my identity. Once again, if you never really know who you are, your perception can become your reality. The idea of recreating my identity threw me into a tailspin, not to mention the lack of cash flow it caused. I talked Roger into extending credit for one last eight-ball (an eighth of an ounce of cocaine) and headed to my other solace: Markus. Happily, coke in hand, we partied all night. The next day was his birthday. I was devastated when he asked me to leave so he could prepare for his date with another woman.

Infidelity was a pattern for Markus. He repeatedly violated my trust, and I had caught him with other women numerous times. His response was always the same: "They don't mean anything to me, baby. I love you." Because my concept of love was based on performance, this was another blow to my confidence. I kept trying to make him give me what he could not, what no man could: value.

Up to this point I was determined to make him love me at all costs, but this episode put me in spiritual and emotional bankruptcy. I was full of rage, and my thinking was only about me; I was self-centered in the extreme. If the world wasn't revolving around me, I felt attacked and wounded. It didn't matter what you were going through; all I could see was me. These feelings entitled me to abuse anyone who crossed my path. Because I was so needy, there was never enough of anything to fill me up. I was manipulative and hostile, and none of it was working. I was burned out, and I could no longer keep going at the same pace. I had made it work for years, but now I was drowning in agony and sorrow. I was a goner, full of heartbreak and totally disillusioned with life.

Overwhelmed by the condition of my life, ravaged by rejection, and confounded by conflict, I searched for a solution; the only one that came to mind was suicide. Heading back to the apartment, I stopped by a convenience store, stole some sleeping pills, and spent my last five bucks on two bottles of wine. As I climbed the steps to that high rise, there was not a morsel of hope in me; the pain I felt in my soul was unbearable. Without Markus's love, I was nothing. I locked myself in my room, shaking, freezing, and sweating, wrapped up in my terry-cloth robe and thinking tortured thoughts. *How can anyone live in this type of turmoil? What happened to the joy in my life? The pain never ends, and loneliness is my constant companion.* Gulping the bottle of wine, I washed down the sleeping pills. *That's it—it's done. Finished.* I just wanted the pain to stop.

The next thing I knew, I was barely coherent in the ER, having a tube pushed down my throat to induce vomit that looked and tasted like black tar. Apparently, in my drunken stupor I had called my mother right after downing the bottle of sleeping pills. This failed attempt to end my life provided me an extended stay in the psych ward. But true to my opportunistic nature I was always looking for a way out. It was easy for me to minimize my consequences, and I had the ability to persuade others to do the same. I duped the psychiatrist with my hard luck story and gained control through seduction. In two days I was out on the street and ready to roll. After my brief stay on the "seventh floor," my parents allowed me to move back in—a decision they would soon regret.

> Addiction is transferable. If you can't escape one way, you find another.

While living with my parents, I was working temp jobs and dating Sean, a longtime family friend. Not only did he provide a bridge to mend family relationships, but we cared deeply for each other, and you know what that means in my world. Any attraction to the opposite sex had to be consummated quickly. Rejection had been my constant companion since kindergarten, and life was not OK unless I felt recognition and approval. I learned quickly how to take men hostage through sex. This offered me the illusion of control that fulfilled my desire to escape. Addiction is transferable. If you can't escape one way, you find another—kind of like whack-a-mole. You hit one, and another pops up.

Temporarily I had replaced my crack addiction with sex, and soon I found out I was pregnant again. Oh, I was irate! So angry! How could I have let this happen? Maybe it was the fact that I never, ever took my birth-control pills on a regular basis. I could rationalize anything I wanted by telling myself I would deal with the consequences later. This newly discovered information was going to throw a wrench into our lifestyle. Both Sean and I liked the way things were. This new obstacle was more than either of us were ready for. We both were living at home with our parents, barely supporting ourselves. Because we did care for each other, there was some talk about possibly keeping the baby, but that soon dissipated as reality crept in. So here I went again: another abortion. I hated it. It hurt, and it was expensive. At least this time I had someone who offered support during and after the procedure.

This abortion proved to be more complicated than the others. After the abortion was performed, late that night I began to have excruciating pain and increased bleeding. I had no choice but to tell my mother, who was shocked. Luckily my father was out of town on business; I knew he wouldn't approve of what I had done. I called the emergency line at the clinic in DC where the procedure was performed, and they sent me to a hospital in Virginia. My poor mother took me to the hospital miles away, even though she didn't like to drive at night or on the Washington Beltway. There it was discovered that the abortion had not been complete; a D & C procedure would have to be performed. Dilation and curettage is a surgical procedure in which the cervix is dilated so that the uterine lining can be scraped to remove abnormal tissues. This was more extensive than any prior experience I had had with abortion. This abortion stuff was more than I had bargained for and was becoming increasingly more troublesome. Now my parents had confirmation about my sex life and that I had gotten an abortion. But like most things, we never discussed it again. Maybe if we didn't talk about it, it didn't exist.

During this time I started to secretly rendezvous with my addictions—Markus and cocaine—and things began to fall apart. For the next two years I searched for a geographic cure. I was still sleeping with Sean but unable to give up Markus and cocaine. My first attempt at this new cure was moving to Manhattan with my former roommate Gabi. Next, I moved to Pennsylvania with my eighty-year-old grandmother and then finally back to Maryland with my parents. None of these moves panned out.

Deep inside I knew that I had to quit using cocaine—it was the culprit in all my problems. It took all my money, destroyed my relationships, and was eating my soul. But in order for me to quit smoking crack, I would have to give up Markus; and two addictions were just too hard to quit at once. For nights upon end I tossed and turned with the idea of breaking free, for good this time. But I was too weak to be on my own. In order for me to really move on, I would need to have something to fill the whole in my heart that would be left by Markus. It would have to be someone or something that was of equal stature. At the moment, that looked like Sean.

Finally, I was ready to leave Markus and cocaine behind—the price was too high to continue associating with either one. Sean and I decided to pack up his Caddy and head to Florida. Being with Sean in a new place was going to be my solution. Although my intentions were honorable, we weren't in Florida a week before my craving to rekindle the love of my life took hold.

This making a new life for ourselves wasn't working. With some research, it wasn't too difficult to find where street drugs were sold—I just scanned the local Clearwater newspaper for drug distribution arrests, the location was there in black and white. Just one hit off that crack pipe was all I needed. Except that one is too many and a thousand is never enough. I hid my drug use from Sean for weeks. Then one day out of the blue, with the help of a private investigator, Markus showed up at the door. He had come to get his woman, and oh, how my heart jumped! Leaving a note on the table, I said goodbye to Sean and Florida to return to what I knew and loved best—my addictions.

The only thing that geography cured in me was the desire to run. I had now seen that when I moved, my problems were there waiting for me. Changing locations may have an initial influence on your thinking, but it doesn't last. Without help, addiction is too much for us. What I was beginning to understand was that my outsides will never fix my insides.

No one I knew pursued cocaine like I did, except Markus. He was willing to go to any length to keep us high. One thing I didn't know was that my "relocating" had created a sense of betrayal in Markus. He said he could no longer trust me. Ironic, coming from the man who flagrantly flaunted his affairs with other women in my face. But this is when the monster of violence within him truly began to rear its ugly head. I felt like if I just loved him enough and if I did everything he asked, I would find the security in our relationship that I craved. But it wasn't working; I had to find a way to gain some type of control. I was doing the exact same thing I had always done but expecting a different result. Today I know that is the definition of insanity.

> What I was beginning to understand was that my outsides will never fix my insides.

When we came back from Florida I moved in with Markus. Soon after I got a job as a bartender at an upscale "gentleman's club" called Archibald's. This was yet another coping mechanism, one that opened the door to a group of people who lived life intensely on the edge. This atmosphere full of beautiful naked women provided a plethora of men, booze, and drugs. Markus loved the money and cocaine I would come home with. Partying all night and through most of the day took its toll, and I found it increasingly difficult to get up and go to work. After several no-shows I was fired.

Not long after, I discovered I was pregnant again and Markus was the father. This would be the solution to our problems. The "white picket fence" fantasy came alive. Maybe being pregnant would end my addiction to crack cocaine, and a baby would heal my relationship with Markus. Finally, I could see a way out, maybe even a normal life. Markus would love me. He would have to take care of me and the baby. I just had to find the right time to tell him.

I decided upon a night when I knew we didn't have any money so we wouldn't be getting high. Nervously I broached the subject, and out of my mouth flew, "I'm pregnant, and I want to keep the baby!"

He wasn't angry. In a reversal of my conversation years ago with Ronnie, this time it was the father of the child who simply said, "No, we can't. I am not ready for that kind of responsibility, and I'm not sure I want to be tied to you the rest of my life anyway." He told me to get an abortion, asking how much money I would need.

I knew just how much I would need, of course. "One-hundred and ninety dollars," I said.

Markus shook his head and laughed. "You better find one of those dudes you've been screwing to give you some money, cause you're not getting it from me, and you're not having that baby!"

The problem was, at that time, I wasn't having sex with anyone but him. *Why did he always think the worst of me? Why couldn't he just love me?* After a few phone calls, I was able to beg and borrow $150, and Markus was generous enough to give me another $50, plus $10 to cover the cab ride.

Staying away from the Planned Parenthood clinic where I had my previous abortion that ended in serious medical complications, I journeyed back to the former Planned Parenthood clinic that performed my second abortion—that one went quick and easy. These folks knew what they were doing.

While sitting in the waiting room, I began to daydream about keeping the baby. *What if I say I got the abortion and don't really do it? What if I tell my parents I want to keep this baby and raise it? That will never work!* As soon as the thoughts came for a different solution than abortion, they quickly left. The nurse calling my name, "Lisa Kratz," startled me back into reality. The inevitable was imminent; I had to go through with the abortion. Gently yet firmly, the nurse guided me by my arm into the procedure room, and I knew what would happen from there. About an hour later, after a cup of orange juice and some cookies, I walked to the street corner and caught a cab back to Northeast DC where Markus lived.

After I paid the cab driver, the walk to his front door seemed like an eternity. *Why was I so emotional?* I wondered. *Life is not OK! I have nothing left to hang over Markus. Now what?* To my surprise, Markus opened the door and gently guided me upstairs. He caressed my hair and brought me food as we lay in bed together through the night. Somewhere deep inside I wanted to believe that maybe this was a turning point for us, and it turned out I was I right—only not in the way I had imagined.

When I awoke the next day, he had already gotten up. I rolled over and pulled myself out of bed to make my way to the bathroom. There on the floor next to the door was an 8" x 10" framed baby picture of Markus. On it was a sticky note that read, "Why did you kill me?"

15

KATHY

The Tipping Point

"There can be as much value in the blink of an eye
as in months of rational analysis."

~Malcolm Gladwell

Frozen and numb, I stood motionless holding the tethered olive green receiver to my ear. The words that came out of my mouth felt robotic and forced. "What?! Oh, Mom and Dad. I'm so sorry. I'm so sorry. Are you OK?" I was stammering, operating in my default mode. Don't feel—focus on someone else. "What happened? What happened?" The explanation that followed seemed incomprehensible—something that only happened on TV. On a deserted road outside of town my brother had been murdered, execution style, shot three times in the back of the head. The police had found him late the night before.

In that moment, the façade of my ideal world fragmented. A few more words were exchanged, and I slowly laid the receiver back in its cradle. *What do I do now? I don't know what to do. What do I do next? That's right, they said to call Dave and have him come home from work.*

When he arrived, he took the baby out of my arms, and I just stood there as he wrapped me in a long hug. I stumbled upstairs, changed out of my workout clothes, and stood in the shower under the steamy downpour until the water ran cold. Hidden in that cascade, the tears began. I sobbed and sobbed and sobbed. Something inside broke open that afternoon; a well of deep emotion, silenced for years, suddenly spilled over. I anguished over Steve facing his last moments so alone. Pain wrenched my heart as I imagined his terror facing such violence.

Then another realization washed over me. *Oh, God. I thought we'd have more time! Now we'll never figure all this out. What a waste! What a waste! I thought we'd have more time.*

That evening, with profound disappointment, we trudged up the cement porch steps of my parents' house. We opened the door and walked into a sea of grieving family and friends. People surrounded us with tearful hugs and words of comfort.

"Steve loved you so much."

"He was so close to you."

"He was so involved in your lives."

Stunned and confused, I just nodded as I strained to digest what they were telling me. Here I'd spent the afternoon agonizing over a door that had slammed shut on ever experiencing the ideal friendship I'd imagined was possible with him. Love wasn't a question in my mind, but close? Involved?

Only a week earlier he had sat at my kitchen table, just the two of us, when he blurted out, "I'm in a rut. I'm in a rut, and I don't think I'll ever get out. You and Dave have done it right." Looking back at him across the table, any reasonable response escaped me. I sat there dumbfounded and self-conscious. How could he think I had it right when I was the one struggling with all of the "shoulds" I wasn't living up to? He was the one living an adventurous life, on the cutting edge of societal and political evolution. He was genuinely helping disenfranchised people I would never even come into contact with in my protected suburban life. I felt no closer to my answers than he did to his. He was way smarter than I was, nobody's fool, well-informed and free spirited. I envied him. Here he was thinking I had it right? That afternoon, neither of us seemed to possess the ability to reason this out with the other.

Now standing in the living room with all these people I loved and respected, I was bewildered. Fresh off of a conversation with him that was full of angst and disappointment, I was being reassured that life with my brother up to that horrific day had been close and wonderful. Shame flooded me. I had very little confidence in my own thinking and perception; and these people were older, smarter, and more accomplished. In a split second, I concluded that they must be right and I was wrong. Silently I berated myself. *How could I have ever thought otherwise? How could I have so misjudged my relationship with my brother? What is wrong with me?* In that moment I dismissed all of my feelings and took on theirs. Too ashamed to admit what I really thought, I left the gathering that night telling no one and burying my feelings.

The days that followed were a chaotic blur. Steve's murderer was on the loose, and no motive had been established. Without our knowledge, a photographer released a picture of our entire extended family to the newspaper. It appeared the next day on the front page. My husband was livid. My dad was relatively well known, and Dave was suspicious it could have been an attack on the family. He became hypervigilant, fearful for our safety.

In sharp contrast to the adrenaline of the manhunt and the media, I was at the funeral home with my mother, arm in arm, slowly weaving through the showroom of caskets. "I think he would like this one. He always loved pine trees." As anyone knows who has been through that, it was surreal. And heart wrenching. Usually full of energy and cheerful, my mother was now pale and fragile. I couldn't fathom her pain.

Friends drove my sisters and me to a department store to pick out dresses for the service. Dazed, everything seemed drained of color. Decisions were impossible, especially about something as meaningless as clothes. I was grateful for their help. The busy store bustled with people laughing and chatting while they shopped. How could everyone act so normal, as if nothing had happened?

> It was comforting to finally be able to express an emotion that fit the circumstances.

Fresh snow fell the morning of the funeral. The church was packed, and plain-clothed police officers surrounded the perimeter of the building. I cried through the entire service. I cried as person after person offered their condolences in the reception line. I couldn't seem to stop crying. And I didn't want to. Whatever had broken loose in me was there to stay. In a way, I was relieved. Although my heart was wrenched with grief, at least I was actually feeling. It was comforting to finally be able to express an emotion that fit the circumstances. At the snowy graveside huddled together with family, my uncle delivered a consoling message. As if divinely orchestrated, the sun suddenly broke through the heavy clouds, and, perched in a nearby tree, a solitary bird began to sing. One by one we laid tulips on his casket. It was a beautiful and terrible day.

In the months that followed, the police captured Steve's killer and recovered the murder weapon. With a full confession of the crime and the man safely behind bars, our lives began to regain some sense of normalcy. If you have ever suffered through the death of someone you love, you know that every event is marked by their absence that first year. Each celebration is "the first" without the one who is gone. Grief ushered in an unexpected depth to my perspective, and some of my perfectionistic drive mellowed. I found myself savoring daily life with our two preschool-age boys; and we filled our hours with games, reading, hikes, bike rides, and visits to grandparents. Energetic and active, they couldn't wait for their daily wrestling time with their dad. "Pile on, Daddy!" brought a smile to my face and reached all the way to my heart.

Although glad for a new appreciation for what was truly important in the wake of my brother's murder, I still faced one glaring disturbance in my life. Night after night, tormenting nightmares continued to plague me, and I wanted relief. I was desperate for it. Talking to anyone about it, however, just wasn't going to happen because the dreams were so bizarre and I didn't think there was any point. It was embarrassing! I didn't know anyone else who had this problem. I'd just have to manage.

I would soon learn that relinquishing denial in one area of life can start to reveal other hidden realities. My fantasy of an ideal, protected life had already been fractured by my brother's violent death. One afternoon, I sat sipping coffee with a good friend of the family. She was a beautiful, tall southern woman with a deep voice and a soothing drawl. Having lost a sibling herself, she was very concerned about how I was recovering. Her attention was especially refreshing because often in the wake of the death of a young person—my brother was only thirty—the focus goes almost solely to the parents, and the siblings are an afterthought.

"So, how are y'all really doin', Kathy?"

Her warmth put me at ease, and in the course of our conversation I found myself confiding in her about the inexplicable nightmares and how tired I was most of the time. Her response was so unexpected, it still rings in my memory today.

"Honey, that's not normal. You don't have to live that way. I have a friend I think you should talk to."

How life changing that simple phrase turned out to be! Often it is the unlikely person who speaks into our lives, the unexpected source. From anywhere, God can send us a message that changes the course of our lives, especially in an atmosphere of love. Love freed me to receive those words. I don't have to live this way. Hope that something better was possible for me seeped into my soul. The sudden revelation of unexpected hope was in itself a tremendous gift from God.

I had lived so long with the secret shame that there was something very wrong with me, that it was my fault, that I must be fundamentally flawed. A counterfeit identity had obscured my true identity. I didn't know that we are each born with a sort of spiritual DNA inside us, a seed that contains an imprint of the very image of God. This seed holds the fruit of spiritual awareness, an awareness that awakens our greatest possible and most fulfilling destiny. I was about to be awakened.

And so it happened that a few trustworthy individuals came to our house to meet with my husband and me. Because of my southern friend's kindness I found the courage to open up about the persistent nightmares. While we sat around in our living room, we simply asked God to help me understand why. There were no psychologists or clergy. Not a single person suggested or even hinted at possible reasons. We were just trying to figure this out together. So it was a shock to me when flashes of memories from my childhood of multiple incidents of molestation surfaced. I recalled with sickening clarity being sexually assaulted when I was away from my parents. A friend ran and brought back a bucket while I sat retching in shock, unable to move. *Oh my God, oh my God! How could I forget this? This can't be happening. Oh my God!*

I had retained some memory of every incident that came to the forefront of my mind, but I had never known how to process the fragments of these traumatic events. Over the next few weeks the nauseating reality settled in. First Steve's death and now this! My world was reeling again.

I didn't have any doubt that the events and images I remembered were authentic. They lined up solidly with circumstances that brought on panic attacks as a child, such as the molestation that occurred at the hands of a gymnastics coach at the YMCA. Even so, I called my sister closest to me in age and asked her about another one of the memories.

> One source of shame in my life finally received some grace.

"Do you remember something happening to us on that playground under the slide?"

Her short reply came over the line. "Yes, I do."

"You didn't forget it?" I asked incredulously.

"No, I've always known something happened there."

I had also known "something bad" had happened there, but it wasn't until now that I made sense out of the pieces I had remembered. I was completely baffled. How was it possible to "forget" parts of traumatic events? This was back in the day before Dr. Phil, and recognition of dissociation from memories due to trauma was only just beginning to be commonly discussed. I'd certainly never heard of it! Some of the same self-accusation haunted me again. *What is wrong with you? How could you have forgotten something as horrible as sexual abuse? Why didn't you tell anyone? Why didn't you do anything to stop it? Why didn't you protect your sister?*

In spite of these tormenting thoughts, to my relief and astonishment the terrors at night faded away as I brought this reality into the light of day. No more waking up screaming. For the first time in over twenty years I regularly slept through the night. My husband was finally getting a full night's sleep too! In addition, I quit blaming myself for being lazy. One source of shame in my life finally received some grace. When I realized the reason I hadn't had energy was because I had been sleep deprived, I became a little less hard on myself.

With all this information and understanding of why I had lived so long being fearful, exhausted, and misunderstood, the anger came. In fact, I was livid. Why hadn't I been protected? Usually warm, open, and affectionate with my parents, I now withdrew and clammed up. I was well aware that they were hurt by my new aloofness and in the dark about the reason, but I wasn't ready to talk. Dave and I finally called a meeting in the presence of a licensed counselor and a third party to tell them about the abuse. It did not go over well. My thinking was, we've got a serious problem here in our family, and it needs to be dealt with. But it was a huge blow for them. It had only been a year since they'd lost their son, and now I'm sure they must have felt like they were losing their daughter.

As the dust settled it became clear that they were skeptical of what I was recounting. This came as another shock to me. I couldn't believe it! I felt like these people I had relied on my whole life were betraying me. I too had lost my brother, and now I was losing them. I felt rejected, indignant, and bewildered. Stubbornly, I kept trying to convince them to accept the reality of these events in my life. And that wasn't working—we had completely different perspectives.

Just as Lisa was trying to get her value from Markus, I too was trying to get validation from a place it couldn't come from. What I didn't realize and couldn't admit to myself was that I had set up my parents as my god—a role no human is meant to play—desperately trying to restore my sense of security through them. It was much more enticing for me to focus on someone else rather than deal with the damage in my own soul. Although I wasn't aware of it then, I'd been siphoning much of my identity and security from other people my whole life. I didn't know any other way to live. I wanted someone else to be my outside fix to an inside problem.

During the next couple of years I started meeting with a counselor, trying to make sense of it all. I knew absolutely nothing about recovering from this kind of trauma. Working through the effects of such appalling and humiliating experiences was grim, and many times I felt ugly and unlovable. That's what sexual abuse will do to a psyche, make the victim turn on herself in disgust. At least self-blame gives an illusion of control in a repulsive situation, even if the fault is taken off of the perpetrator. The victim's image of herself can become drastically distorted. Sitting in my car after one particularly painful counseling session in which I had talked frankly about one of the violating events, I checked my makeup in the visor mirror. Startled to see my slender face in the reflection, I realized that in my mind's eye I had pictured myself as extremely overweight. It was like looking at "before and after" pictures you see in weight loss ads. This distortion was entirely unconscious; I had no idea I was doing it.

As the months went on I was slowly healing, separating out the feelings from the facts. The world as I had seen it had altered so drastically in just a few short years. I was working hard at orienting myself to this new reality and dealing with the nitty gritty work of abuse recovery, but I hadn't even scratched the surface of my deeply rooted habit of perfectionism and comparison. I wanted so badly for outer performance to give me security and make me feel loved. I still clung to the idea that if my family would just validate me, all the other pieces would magically come together and I'd be as good as new. I just wanted to hear, "This must be so hard for you. Let's work through this together." But that wasn't happening.

When my husband was offered a job across the country I was ready for a change. Maybe a new location, a change of scenery, would be the answer to mend how broken my world felt. We could start over. That's what I needed: a geographic cure.

16

LISA

The High Cost of Freedom

"There is no easy walk to freedom anywhere,
and many of us will have to pass through the valley
of the shadow of death again and again
before we reach the mountaintop of our desires."

~Nelson Mandela

Something in me changed the morning Markus left that picture and note. Something was lost. All Markus wanted to do was hurt me, shame me, and degrade me. This was his way of making me feel like he was the only one who would want me. It was a game of control. In the face of Markus's betrayal and cruelty, a wall went up around my emotions that would remain for years. This wall allowed me to shut out anything and anyone who had the power to hurt me. Of course, it also shut out anyone who wanted to help me. If you do anything long enough to escape your feelings, soon the escape becomes the habit. All that was important to me was getting high at all costs. Soon I would see just how exorbitant that price was.

Not long after that abortion, the bank caught up with Markus and foreclosed on his house where we had been living together. Now we were homeless, which made it difficult to find employment and left us with a lot of time on our hands for creating new money-making schemes.

When I had been employed at Archibald's I shared with Markus that many girls I worked with exchanged sex for drugs. Remembering this he verbally intimidated me to make calls to our regular dealers to persuade them to front me some coke. Both of us knew the only way this could happen was for me to barter—cocaine in exchange for sex. I wasn't crazy about the idea, but these guys were familiar, and they were responding to my invitation. Quickly, through physical aggression, Markus's requests progressed into demands to do whatever was necessary to get a fix. When night fell, I would hit the street near our hotel room and knew not to come back empty handed.

I was stuck with Markus now, for better or for worse. For the better part of a year we were part of a community of literally thousands of homeless drug addicts who lived in rent-by-the-hour hotel rooms at night. During the day we wandered aimlessly through the city, riding the subway in the winter to stay warm and lounging in the park during the summertime. But as the sun set we would pay for whatever portion of an hour we could afford, retreat to our hotel room, and begin our evening ritual.

I would be forced out on the streets to earn some money. He waited anxiously for me to return with either the money or the crack. He would be agitated until he took that first hit. Then Markus would immediately turn violent, threatening to put me out in the street alone and then beat me until I begged him to let me stay. And I endured it all for the tiny little rock of crack cocaine. I was in a no-win situation, and life without a mind-altering substance was more than I could fathom. As I lay on the floor, battered from his abuse, I knew I had to find a way out.

Although he pushed me to the street, forcibly pimping me out, using me so he could stay high himself, he never took the responsibility for this. He always referred to what he demanded I do as my way of being able to have sex with other men. As if that was on my bucket list. When I would bring home the money after hours on the street, he would slap me around for what he had sent me to do, never mentioning the fact that if I didn't hit the streets there would be hell to pay and I owed the bill. It never seemed to cross his mind that the money I made would go up in smoke exhaled from his lungs.

After pursuing this money-making line of employment and violent lifestyle for close to a year, I was tired of being used up, beat up, and tossed out. So I had to come up with a new plan—a much more civilized idea, one that would allow me my dignity . . . so we initiated a check-writing scheme. However, in the midst of operating this brilliant ruse, I found myself pregnant yet again.

My firm philosophy about pregnancy was that I would not bring a baby into this world because my life was such a mess. And I was not willing to sacrifice my only solace, cocaine, in order to give birth to a healthy baby. Just as Dr. Nathanson predicted, after four abortions the point could be made that I was using abortion as a means of birth control. In the midst of such daily chaos, my best intentions got me nowhere. I tried to get and stay on the pill, but being homeless, that fifteen dollars a month was better spent on anything else—especially cigarettes or booze. Besides, all my days ran together—beginning late at night and ending when the sun came up. Then there were the benders where I would get no sleep at all for days on end. Through all these experiences, especially the soul-grinding experience of prostitution, I had learned how to block any emotions or second thoughts about my decision to terminate my pregnancies. Especially after the last tormenting post-abortion experience with Markus, I told myself to *suit up, shut up, and show up*. No room for thinking or feeling about abortion now.

The logistics of this current abortion, a year and a half later, proved to be a bit more complicated than the rest. Having no real, steady income was a huge hurdle; but I had to keep this from Markus, and that would be dif-ficult. Fear was the overwhelming fac-tor in keeping this secret.

> Desensitization is just one of the many mind changes caused by addiction.

Even though the stage had changed, the actors were the same. I thought if I got off the street, Markus would be less violent. I was wrong. The beatings were getting worse. Instead of just using his hands, he began to hold knives and daggers to my throat, strangling me until I passed out. When you start using cocaine it is an aphrodisiac; but like many other things that start out good, it can take a turn for the worse. Desensitization is just one of the many mind changes caused by addiction. You feel less pleasure, and that creates a need for different stimulation for satisfaction—it's as if you become numb to what excited you previously. Of course, there are neurological, brain-chemistry reasons for this as well as psychological ones; but I knew none of that at the time—nor would it have made any difference. Markus was becoming more sexually violent. For years, after violent episodes he would be remorseful and beg for forgive-ness, but that time had long passed. I was terrified of him—too intimidated to leave yet afraid to stay. I knew that if he found out I was pregnant, he might once and for all lose his mind and kill me.

The fact that my life was literally hanging in the balance on whether this new money-making venture worked certainly pushed me to be creative. Generally, addicts and alcoholics are some of the sharpest, most driven people alive; it's just that we are focused on unhealthy pursuits. If we could turn our destructive determination around, we could conquer the world.

Relieved, Markus and I had hit the big time: our genius check-writing scheme was working. Although we were still living in the same hotel, we were able to rent the room by the day instead of the hour. This provided enough cash and security for me to sneak away for forty-eight hours. Lying to Markus, I told him I was visiting my parents. This enabled me to take care of my problem, my "inconvenience," which I vowed would be the last time. Never mind the fact that just months before I had been in this very same situation swearing it would never happen again. My heart is saddened by how little respect or thought I gave to the life of the baby growing inside me and to my own personhood as a woman. But when you don't even love or value yourself, you don't have the capacity to have compassion or concern for others. I went on with my life unrestrained because the only vision I had was maintaining my high. As the Bible says, without purposeful vision people perish—and that was what I was doing one day at a time.

Our scheme worked for just over six months before the law caught up with me. I was arrested in 1989 in Arlington, Virginia, for forgery and fraud. I was transported via police paddy wagon to the county jail.

Incarceration is a life event that either makes you or "brakes" you. What I mean by that is it can make you into a person who doesn't mind an occasional lock-up, or it can put the brakes on your criminal behavior, compelling some type of change in your life so you don't return again. Incarceration made a believer out of me. It felt more like *One Flew Over the Cuckoo's Nest*. I couldn't come back here, ever. The fact that I could not leave became real after a few days. Days were long and nights even longer. Not only was my freedom gone, but also there was absolutely no privacy, not even when using the toilet. The food was bad, and the permeating smell of oppression was overwhelming. Noise is constant behind bars, twenty-four hours a day, seven days a week—never any quiet. And then there's the intimidation and violation factor: the snitches, the beggars, and those who are looking for sexual release. These are basically the same factors you face on the street, but out there you have a choice to flee.

Although the degradation of being locked up was overwhelming, greater was the fear and humiliation of coming face to face with myself. This was the first time in fifteen years that I had gone any considerable length of time without drugs or alcohol. My bond was set at $10,000 dollars and I could have been bailed out through a bondsman for $1,000. But I knew that if Markus happened to get his hands on $1,000 he sure wasn't going to use it to bail me out of jail. He would do with it what I would do if I had it, of course. So there I sat for close to a year.

In jail you have a lot of time to think. It's like a time warp, like the outside world stands still. When you have anesthetized and suppressed your emotions and feelings for so long, it is difficult and somewhat overpowering when they all coming rushing back simultaneously. To say I was uncomfortable with my feelings is an understatement; frankly, I did not know the person who was living in my skin. *Look where I ended up—how could I have let this drug thing get so out of hand?* My thoughts were a mass of conflicting ideas and emotions. I was scared, and I had no idea what the future held for me. Unbeknownst to me, much later down the road I would have the opportunity to reflect on how valuable the lessons of incarceration would be and just how truly beautiful it is to be sober.

About a month after I was locked up, the on-duty officer called me out to her desk. She was a beautiful black woman with perfectly groomed hair, bright red nails and lips, and a soothing yet direct voice. "Lisa," she said, "what are you doing here?" I began to recite my charges, and she interrupted. "No, baby, not your charges . . . what are *you* doing here? There is more for you in life than this."

> In order to experience change we must be willing to admit fault, take responsibility, and put that awareness into action.

I thought, *Are you talking to me?* She went on to say that she had been an officer for over ten years, and she could spot someone quickly who was not fulfilling their purpose, someone who had just fallen prey to their feelings and gotten into something that enveloped their life. "Many women are satisfied with low-level living. For weeks I have been watching you, and I have to say you are not the type of woman who belongs here. There is a bigger plan for you. Your job is to find out what that plan is and get in line with it."

I was shocked. *She must be delusional. Doesn't she know what kind of woman I am? The worst of the worst, that's the kind of woman I am: a liar, a cheat, a junkie, and a whore. The only reason anybody wanted me around was what I could do for them. Other than that, I don't have much to offer.* But that blessed officer saw something deeper. I thanked her, but I didn't really know if gratitude was what I was feeling. I think disbelief would be more accurate.

When I returned to my bunk, our conversation opened my mind to new and different possibilities. *Maybe there is a way to break this self-fulfilling prophecy I have created for myself. What if there is a better way to live? Maybe one day I could get off drugs.* But I was in a pattern of negative thinking. I still held out for my Prince Charming—someone to sweep me off my feet and take me away from my life. Unable to contemplate how I might change myself, I focused on how I should step up my game, get rid of my sleazy image, and regain my classy, sexy vibe. Maybe this would eliminate all the shame I felt on the inside and allow me the emotional safety and ability to please a real man. This plan was still in the realm of fantasy, but it did offer a vision that was a step up from the life I had been living—with Markus I didn't even have the expectation of physical safety, let alone financial stability.

I was aware of something else after my conversation with the officer too: I actually felt hopeful and good about myself. It had been a long time since I had experienced those feelings, and I liked it. But again I was living from extreme to extreme. One minute without any hope at all; and in the next, at the first scent of possibility to change, conjuring up schemes to get a man. Hope mixed with fantasy will never produce reality. In order to experience change we must be willing to admit fault, take responsibility, and put that awareness into action. I wasn't quite there yet.

I went into that jail feeling like discarded trash, but while I was there a seed of hope was dropped into my heart by someone I didn't know and would never see again. Sometimes it is in the darkest places that a ray of light shines through. Today I remain eternally grateful for that officer who took the time to speak positive affirmation into my life. However, if a seed is not watered or fertilized it can lay dormant for many seasons.

Markus was waiting at the door when I was released from jail. We walked across the street to the Pizza Hut and drank a pitcher of beer that I paid for with a bad check. Within two hours we were back at a fleabag motel, crack in hand. The name calling and accusations began to flow. In moments, I was getting my head bashed in and the life kicked out of me for merely being alive. For more than a decade I had experienced many devastating, violent, and shocking things. Individually they were manageable, but collectively they began to infiltrate my spirit. After nearly a year of being clean in jail, and after the somewhat positive thoughts I'd begun to allow myself to think, finally this was the straw that broke the camel's back. In a moment of clarity, I did something I had never done before: with plenty of crack left to smoke, I left that hotel room and never turned back. I went outside and sat on the curb, asking myself over and over, *How did I get here again? How, after being off the streets, away from Markus and cocaine, did I get here again? What is wrong with me? WHY do I keep doing this to myself?*

Today I realize that time does not heal all wounds; it just makes the pain more manageable. Without help it is too much for us; but there is one who has all the help, and that one is God. My concept of God at that time was of a cruel taskmaster who only loved those who were lovely. I thought He was disappointed in me and that He hated me for the person I had become. But desperate people do desperate things. Despite my thoughts about God, I looked up into the sky in total misery and cried out to Him for help!

Many people ask what does it take for someone to hit rock bottom? My answer is that everyone has a different threshold for pain and misery. I had hit many lows in my life, but I was resilient, obviously with a high ability to withstand pain. Many times I said to myself, *If such-and-such ever happens I will know I have hit bottom,* only to rationalize it when that scenario would present itself. But all these devastating circumstances led me to a deep, dark valley and helped me come to the end of me and the beginning of God. I knew I was at the end when drugs and alcohol didn't provide any relief; they quit working. One good thing about being at that point is that it can't get any worse.

When you hit bottom you either change or die. Every blow that I received in life is what got me to say enough is enough. That is what I needed to experience to propel me into change. But just like everything else in my life, I wanted recovery on my terms. I needed an immediate solution to a problem that took me a lifetime to create. God's time is not our time, and because He didn't work on my timetable I took things into my own hands, as usual.

Contemplating what to do next, I went to the payphone on the corner and made a few calls. An old using buddy and his wife gave me one night's reprieve. The next day, after a hot shower and a clean set of clothes, I headed out seeking a job. Luckily there was an Italian restaurant on the corner that was in need of an experienced waitress. This was before smartphones and immediate background checks—these days, I wouldn't have been so lucky. After a few nights of sleeping in garages and backyards and using the Exxon station bathroom sink as my shower, I earned enough cash tips for a hotel room. Everything in me was yearning to resort to what was familiar, the old patterns and behaviors. But even then God was looking out for me.

With too much time on my hands, I knew I had to find some new people to hang with. This is when I started spending time in the fringes of the rooms of twelve-step recovery. I attended meetings sporadically, getting there late, never sharing during the hour, and leaving as soon as the meeting was over. I wasn't interested in getting too chummy with any of the group members. Although I saw the light of optimism in the concept of recovery, I wasn't ready to embrace it myself. In my opinion, the group members were a little too invested in this whole meeting thing. I checked in every now and then but was just not completely ready to give myself to the program of recovery.

Simultaneously, I also entered into a relationship that got me off the street and into a somewhat normal living situation. But I soon came to the realization that I wasn't living; I was just surviving. The people changed, the set was rearranged; but the same gnawing emptiness filled my soul. For most of my life, my pattern of thinking had remained the same. I was worthless, shameful, and outcast. Everybody else had figured out how to live life successfully but me. Sound familiar? It's the same pattern of faulty thinking Kathy was laboring under. We are all more alike than we ever imagined.

I kept falling deeper and deeper into the pattern of self-hatred. The same pain and self-loathing voice that told me so many years ago I was a bad little girl sounded like a megaphone in my mind. These thoughts would often take me back to that lonely day when I stood on that bridge contemplating suicide at the age of five. But finally, I was beginning to see it. I was tired of hating who I was. This is when I truly knew something had to change—a part of me had to die so the new me could be resurrected.

17

BERNIE

"Show Me the Money"

"No woman wants an abortion
as she wants an ice cream cone or a Porsche.
She wants an abortion as an animal,
caught in a trap, wants to gnaw off its own leg.
Abortion is a tragic attempt to escape
a desperate situation by an act of violence and self-loss."

~Frederica Mathewes-Green

Dr. Bernard Nathanson's passion for abortion was born out of his best intentions. Unlike many of us, he followed through on his intentions with action and dedication—and eventually obsession. He worked tirelessly until his passion became a reality. Determination and an absolute belief in the rightness of his cause drove him at neck-breaking speed through the campaign, the legal process, and then establishing medically adequate abortion clinics. But by the time *Roe v. Wade* was decided, Dr. Nathanson was worn out, disillusioned, and overwhelmed with doubts. He left the trenches of the abortion industry after being introduced to the humanity of the unborn through the ultrasound, and his careful study of fetology eventually led to his total rejection of abortion.

How could he have so missed the mark? His intentions were altruistic. He just wanted to help women in poverty faced with unplanned pregnancies. But in his passion he could see only one solution. The reality is he had never been open to considering anything but abortion. In his mind there were no alternatives to achieve the same end. As he later reflected, "When one is caught up in revolutionary fervor, one simply does not want to hear the other side and filters out evidence without realizing it."[1]

Have you ever wanted something so badly that you are willing to do anything to get it, even if it isn't good for you? Trying harder and exerting more energy into forcing the same solution even though it hasn't worked before? What does it take for us to finally open our eyes and consider another possibility? For Kathy it was a violent death and facing childhood abuse. For Lisa it was being beaten one last time. For Bernie it was seeing the dark underworld of abortion.

We live in a prove-it-to-me society. "Show me the money," that famous prove-it-to-me line from the movie *Jerry McGuire*, became an instant national catchphrase. There is wisdom in the idea that we shouldn't just believe something on blind faith. But on the other hand, in the infamous parody of *Dragnet's* Joe Friday, "Just the facts ma'am" are overlooked and manipulated to support a point of view. So which is it?

Abortion is a volatile subject, and we've all been barraged with statistics from both sides of the debate. Dr. Nathanson was the king of abortion fact manipulation, and because of that he knew how important it was that viable statistics supported his change of perspective. Stories captivate people, and sometimes we are tempted to skip statistics. But these statistics are more than just numbers and ratios on a page. They uncover the real story of abortion buried under slogans and rhetoric. This chapter is about real stories, real lives. And Lisa Kratz Thomas is one of those stories.

In Washington, DC, stands a well-deserved, hauntingly beautiful memorial commemorating the fifty-eight thousand lives lost in the Vietnam War. It looms ten feet high and stretches five hundred feet long. If we were to honor the precious lives of innocent children lost to abortion, that Abortion Holocaust Memorial Wall standing ten feet high would be over eighty-one *miles* in length and display fifty-seven *million* names. In America, we are literally walking around in a land haunted by ghosts as a result of legalized abortion. In a paraphrase of his conversation with Sir William Liley, the brilliant father of fetology, Bernard Nathanson said Liley claimed this: "For a generation that prefers scientific fact to philosophy, you would think this new information about the unborn baby would create a new respect for the welfare of the life in the womb. Instead, around the world we find a clamoring for the destruction of the fetus as a cure-all for every social and personal problem."[2]

Bernie Nathanson's fervor for legalized abortion buried and silenced his ethical convictions. He was willing to turn a blind eye to the Hippocratic Oath in which he had vowed to do no harm. He was willing to lie, repeatedly. He and his inner circle concocted and fed false statistics and deceptive slogans to the American public. They repeated the lies often enough until they were accepted as truth. "Until 1973 I was sold a bill of goods. No—let me be honest—I was selling a bill of goods."[3] He threw in his lot with a master manipulator, Lawrence Lader, who indoctrinated him with the virtues of abortion on demand. He then turned around and sold it to America, who bought it hook, line, and sinker.

As Lisa would one day learn in that pivotal radio interview, the number of women's deaths associated with illegal abortions was grossly exaggerated. She was furious to find out that this smug group of revolutionaries literally laughed in sarcasm while inventing slogans to sell their lies—slogans that directly affected her own life, years later:

"Women must have control over their own bodies."

"Who decides? You decide!"

"Abortion is a personal decision between a woman and her doctor."

"Will women decide, or will the politicians and bureaucrats in Washington?"

> Another source of confusion over abortion "rights" is that abortion has never been a constitutional right.

"Freedom of choice—a basic American right!"[4]

Bernie Nathanson didn't believe these slogans or the trumped up statistics, but there were a lot of things he did believe, only later to drastically change his mind. This is in part his story; and if anyone is qualified to educate on abortion, it is certainly Bernie Nathanson.

His campaign worked all too well. These days our society has taken for granted that abortion is "a woman's right to choose." Let us remember that this was a slogan created by those men brainstorming around that table.

Another source of confusion over abortion "rights" is that abortion has never been a constitutional right. *Roe v. Wade* was a Supreme Court decision. This confusion has perpetuated a mentality that some human beings are disposable. Another way to look at this so-called right is to recall that with every right still comes responsibility. Americans have a constitutional right to bear arms, but we cannot exercise this right and commit murder.

Bernie started believing in abortion during his residency because he was convinced abortion would improve the lives of impoverished women, decreasing their poverty level. He envisioned that women living in poverty would have the option to end an unwanted pregnancy and improve their situation. He considered this a rare and emergency-based situation. It sounds reasonable: one less mouth to feed could lead to greater freedom and better opportunities for the mother. He never intended abortion to be used as birth control, which is exactly what it is being used as today.

The reality is that impoverished women are more likely to engage in unprotected sex and more likely to have repeated abortions. This is in spite of contraceptive education and knowledge.[5] In 1973 an estimated 12 percent of women had repeated abortions. That number rose to 40 percent by 1983.[6] So why is this a problem? Multiple studies have shown that the economic status of women deteriorates when abortions are repeated. Women with higher incidence of abortion are more likely to be divorced and on welfare. They are less likely to be enrolled as a student. In other words, abortion is not opening the way for a better life.[7]

Abortion also increases the likelihood of breaking up existing romantic relationships, and because of this the woman is often reduced to a single income situation instead of dual income. Only 10 percent of women having abortions marry the child's father, and only 20 percent continue to live with the father in the years following the abortion.[8]

A high percentage of post-abortive women intentionally get pregnant again to replace the child that was lost through their abortion. Most of these pregnancies also end in abortion, which leads one to wonder about the psychological trauma involved. If abortion is supposed to eliminate a mere problem, why do women try to replace what was only a "fetus"?[9]

Again, in his admirable zeal to improve the conditions of women's physical health, Bernie Nathanson never considered the psychological fallout from abortion. He believed that abortion was simply a surgical procedure, one that could be performed safely and with excellence. What psychological effect could the professional removal of a mass of tissues possibly have on a woman? That is, unless the aborted fetus possessed the same full humanity as the mother herself? In that case, she would indeed be dealing with the death of a child—and at her own choosing.

Post-Abortion Syndrome (PAS) is a collection of symptoms experienced by women who have had an abortion. They include guilt, anxiety, avoiding children or pregnant women, suppressed emotions, depression, suicidal thoughts, fear of infertility, replacement pregnancies, trouble bonding with present or future children, anger, difficulty in relationships, eating disorders, and substance abuse.[10] These symptoms are real, and they are pathological—they occur regularly enough to suggest that something is wrong and that a pattern is at work.

The American Medical Association refuses to give credibility to PAS. And yet the massive amount of evidence documenting the deep psychological trauma following abortion is overwhelming. Suicide attempts skyrocket. Among pregnant women, those who abort are six to seven times more likely to attempt suicide in the following six months and two and a half times more likely in the subsequent eight years than those who carried to term.[11] Among teens, they are ten times more likely to attempt suicide in the following six months than those who haven't had an abortion.[12] For a supposedly low-risk, reasonable solution, these are alarming figures indeed.

Another myth about abortion is the notion of "a woman's choice." In reality, in many cases that simply isn't true. Well over half of all abortions (64%) involve coercion from a parent or partner.[13] This was true for Lisa and many other women as well. The statistic pointing to suicide for pregnant teenage girls is especially alarming. They are often pressured by parents to abort, or never tell their parents out of fear of anger and shame. Numerous teens' mothers have threatened loss of support and insisted on abortion for their pregnant daughters. As a parent, wouldn't you much rather deal with the consequences of an unplanned baby than attend the funeral of your daughter? But these consequences are rarely discussed among proponents of abortion.

The abortion industry confidently presents abortion as having very limited and short-term aftereffects. Planned Parenthood, even with its currently shaky credibility, maintains that "most substantive studies in the last 30 years have found abortion to be a relatively benign procedure in terms of emotional effect—except when pre-abortion emotional problems exist or when a wanted pregnancy is terminated, such as after diagnostic genetic testing."[14] But the evidence screams the opposite. Post-abortive women with no previous emotional problems have higher rates of suicidal behavior, depression, anxiety, substance abuse, and other disorders after abortion.[15] They have a fivefold increase in alcohol and substance abuse, and 39 percent develop eating disorders.[16]

> The statistic pointing to suicide for pregnant teenage girls is especially alarming.

Lisa was the poster child for these statistics. She certainly had other problems as well, but the impact of abortion on her life was tremendous. PAS helps to explain what went wrong in her life, and research shows that "prior psychological problems are more likely to be made worse by abortion, not better."[17] Because of this knowledge, she is now certain this is why she slipped into years of depression, drinking, and freebasing cocaine. She believes all of her dysfunction—the substance abuse, the prostitution, suicide attempt, incarceration, and subsequent abortions—were a large part of the aftermath of the initial abortion in 1979. All of these serious side effects are a huge problem in our country, and we don't even have a clue that they are related to abortion.

Dr. Nathanson also never considered the effects of abortion on subsequent siblings. Tragically, studies have linked previous abortions to an increase in child abuse. Abortion is associated with increased violence and poor maternal bonding with later children due to unresolved trauma.[18] Of course, it would be absurd to conclude that all women who have aborted in the past abuse their children. Certainly that is not the case. Nevertheless, there remains a 144 percent higher risk factor of child abuse than for non-abortive women.[19]

What about the fathers? There are entire organizations dedicated to helping grieving fathers who have had no say in the termination of their children, leaving them with a feeling of loss and of powerlessness. Studies are only recently being conducted on the aftershocks of abortion on post-abortive fathers. Initial findings include difficulty with commitment, relationship struggles, inability to trust friends, rage, addictions and sexual compulsions, nightmares, depression, and fear of rejection.[20]

What about the broader picture? If there's one area that makes us sit up and pay attention it's when something affects our pocketbook. One factor that is seldom talked about is the impact of abortion on the economy. While abortion doctors rake in a hefty side income, an estimated $831 million each year, an average of $500,000 per doctor, the economy as a whole suffers.[21] The economy also suffers from the absence of citizens lost to abortion. So often, abortion is promoted as a financial relief for the mother or the family. But, the reality is that had *Roe v. Wade* never passed, we would have approximately seventeen million more workers contributing to the economy today. With our national debt of $17 trillion, these workers would contribute $400 billion to the economy![22]

And all the while we have infertile couples, many of whom in addition to the grief of not being able to bear children are waiting and waiting for a baby to adopt and love. In the United States, there are up to thirty-six couples in queue to adopt for every one baby placed for adoption.[23] This heart-wrenching, deep longing is repeatedly thwarted as eleven out of every twelve potentially adoptable babies are aborted. Think of the agonizing disappointment of these families who yearn to adopt a child while the expectant mother vetoes any chance of life by choosing abortion. So often we hear, "There just aren't enough resources for all these babies." Yet, if twelve out of twelve babies were carried to term, we would have three couples for each one. Three times the number of adoptive parents for each aborted child! These are wanted children, and there are more than enough to go around.

Sometimes it is hard to imagine what good could come from these desperate situations women find themselves in. There can be great difficulty struggling financially and emotionally to raise a child on your own. But everyone's life has value and purpose. What if one woman's struggles and sacrifice were to produce someone like the next Ben Carson, the renowned pediatric brain surgeon? He was raised by an illiterate single mom.

Undoubtedly, the decision to give a baby up for adoption takes courage. It always requires courage to put your child's needs above your own. Yet think of the woman who gave Steve Jobs a better life through adoption. She had no way of knowing the incredible contribution he would make to society. Across the board, how many Mozarts, Mother Teresas, Thomas Edisons, Michael Jordans, Martin Luther Kings, or Sonia Sotomayors are we missing today because they never had a chance to leave their imprint on society? And that's just to name people who have achieved great things in a public way. But let's not miss a deeper truth at work here. *Every* person is of great value just by being made in the image of the divine Creator, God.

America was founded on the basis of diversity, and we celebrate cultural differences. It is tragic then that in minority communities a higher percentage of babies are aborted.[24] Is it possible that the fact that 78 percent of abortion facilities have been strategically placed in areas with a high minority popula-tions is a contributing factor?[25]

> Women who have had an abortion have a much greater risk of infertility and difficulties during pregnancy.

Bernie crusaded for abortion on demand from a passion to better a woman's overall health. But studies now show that abortion is directly linked to breast cancer. And yet, the American Medical Association beats the drum loudly and repeatedly that there is no conclusive link between abortion and breast cancer. Perhaps we're simply not willing to look at the truth in this country. Twelve out of twelve recent studies conducted in India all showed conclusively that abortion increases a woman's risk for breast cancer. In fact, the Indian studies show a greater link between abortion and breast cancer than any other risk fac-tors, such as advanced age, family history of breast cancer, or barrenness.[26]

Many women desire to have children sometime in their future, but few are aware of how abortion threatens that dream. Women who have had an abortion have a much greater risk of infertility and difficulties during pregnancy. Induced abortion is a surgical procedure, and the potential dangers involved were the primary reason Dr. Nathanson immersed himself in the world of abortion in the first place. In his writings he talks about the major risks of abortion he witnessed firsthand such as hemorrhaging, perforation of the uterus, infection, subse-quent infertility, and even death. He was highly motivated to try to protect women from these terrible outcomes by providing "safe" abortions. In reality, abortion isn't safe. Even if these major complications don't follow, abortion increases the risk of difficulty with subsequent pregnancies and actual infertility.

In an abortion the cervix, uterus, and uterine wall are directly affected. All are vital for future pregnancies. A very common aftereffect of forced dilation is a weakening of the cervix.[27] This can cause serious complications in pregnancy such as hemorrhaging and even death of the mother and/or child during labor.[28] Scarring of the uterine wall is another serious risk involved in abortion. Even a small amount of scarring can result in hormone suppression, menstrual pain and complications, miscarriages, and infertility.[29]

Finally, for years the Centers for Disease Control (CDC) has reported that childbirth-related deaths are higher than abortion-related deaths. In other words, that abortion is safer than childbirth. However, recently the CDC itself has admitted that maternal mortality rates and abortion mortality rates cannot be compared. Their numbers mean nothing. It's like comparing apples to oranges. But in Finland, a country with nationalized health care, it is required to include abortion as a cause of death in their records. Their study unmistakably reveals that deaths from abortion are four times higher than from childbirth.[30]

Dr. Nathanson was so sure that abortion would elevate women's health care, benefiting society. He banked on it, devoted his life to it, and sacrificed his family for it. He couldn't have been any more wrong. He came to understand his grotesquely twisted perspective only a short while after *Roe v. Wade* opened the floodgate to abortion on demand. Facts don't lie. Legalized abortion has left the women of our nation with broken hearts, scarred and diseased bodies, anguished minds, and in many cases even lost lives. Our nation has suffered financially from the loss of millions of productive workers, not to mention the creative minds, inventions, and potential medical cures these aborted children could have given us. We as a nation are suffering the loss of fifty-seven million citizens. "I am compelled to report that the revolution we undertook was an ultimately poisonous dream," Nathanson said. "It all appeared so certain at the time . . . Now in light of the best data . . . that old certainty has vanished forever."[31]

In the face of all this past and ongoing loss of our fellow citizens, what can we possibly do? What hope is there? Kathy's brother, Steve, once told her about having leaned against that Vietnam War Memorial wall and weeping for those precious lost lives. Many who have survived that war and were rehabilitated from its effects have in turn greatly impacted the lives around them. Lisa, who survived and recovered from drug abuse, prostitution, incarceration, and the pain of abortion now reaches out to thousands sharing experience, strength, and hope. And she is just one person. If every person who has chosen abortion had a change of heart like Dr. Nathanson or Lisa, imagine the force for good and contribution these individuals could have for generations to come.

18

BERNIE

Surprised by Restoration

> "Some men, like fish, need to be caught
> by their head. Bernie was such a man."
>
> ~Deacon Keith Fournier

His eyes flew open in the darkness, his body shook; dread constricted his chest, and a cold sweat was on his brow. Groaning, he rolled over to check his clock. Four a.m. He breathed deeply, trying to force the agony away and his body back to sleep. Loneliness engulfed him like the night around him. After what seemed like hours, he reached for his lamp and switched on the light. Only fifteen minutes had passed. A soft glow filled his bedroom, but he felt no warmth as he looked toward a stack of books on his nightstand. St. Augustine's *Confessions* and other writings dealing with sin—which one held the key? Where were his answers hiding, if they existed at all? He sighed, and plucked Augustine from the pile. Opening the worn copy, he dejectedly started reading.

It was 1988, a decade after he'd performed his last abortion. The horror Bernie experienced in the late '70s when he realized that abortion is murder had only grown over the years. His heart carried an unbearable load that was becoming increasingly heavier. He had come to the conclusion that he was suffering from a tormented spirit. For years he had lived free from moral restraint, guided by his own sense of right and wrong. Now he was heavy with guilt, searching for atonement for his wrongs. He had performed abortions on thousands of innocent children, one of whom was his own, had three destroyed marriages, and had failed those he loved most.

Relying heavily on his intellect, he meticulously read and reread renowned philosophers. Bernie had never been persuaded by emotion, and he wasn't about to start now. He was born and bred with a thirst for knowledge. His intelligence, until now, had served him well in quenching that thirst. Sentiment didn't motivate him, but pain certainly did. He was completely out of his depth. He had come to the conclusion that he, an atheist, was dealing with the problem of sin. His sin. For the first time in his adult life, Bernie was having trouble finding a solution to a problem. The writers were brilliant at analyzing sin; but maddeningly, none of them offered a solution. It was crazy-making for him. But having nowhere else to turn, he kept reading, hoping to discover something he might have missed.

The truth was, Bernie wanted to kill himself.[1] As a physician, he could easily put together a lethal cocktail and slip from this world painlessly. After all, suicide ran in his family. His grandfather had hung himself, and his sister had ended her life with a bottle of sleeping pills. His father had even attempted it. Maybe he was just like them. Doomed.

This is one of the most seductive types of deception, one that can hold a powerful, dark sway over us. Many of us have cringed under condemning accusations: "You're coldhearted, just like your father!" "You'll never amount to anything, just like your brother." "Your mother was a drunk, and you'll end up just like her." "You're just like—" fill in the blank. How many of us have believed these accusations? Have you? There's just one little problem with these statements. No one knows the future, except God. Each of us has our own unique journey, full of twists and turns and possibilities.

Bernie Nathanson kept his toxic thoughts to himself, slowly poisoning his own mind and soul with despair. It wasn't his nature to share his deepest thoughts. He did, however, possess the grace to employ one lifesaving tactic: procrastination. He kept putting off killing himself. One day at a time, he talked himself out of it.

Bernie may not have felt any tangible hope of finding an answer to his guilt and pain, but he did have work to do. Countless women were being served through his new gynecological practice. He was in on the cutting edge of advances in fetology. He attended and spoke at numerous pro-life functions. He granted interviews to a variety of publications and radio and television programs. In his "free time" the driven doctor wrote two books and produced two films advocating the end of abortion. He was a busy man, biding his time, hoping to somehow make amends for the bloody terror he had unleashed on innocent and unsuspecting babies. The torment that awoke him in the night drove him to action.

Bernie saw a glimpse of the terror of the unborn in abortion during the making of *The Silent Scream* and *Eclipse of Reason*. Dr. Nathanson was a haunted man. Each attempt to put a halt to what he had, in part, unleashed seemed to have no effect. Nothing seemed to be changing. The runaway steamroller of abortion was leaving a bloody trail across our nation. Bernie spiraled silently into ever increasing despair. He saw no hope for the future.

And what about those of us watching the hours tick by, enduring heart-wrenchingly painful circumstances? Lisa did this for years. She wasn't living; in fact she was barely existing and hating what she had become—a failure, an outcast, a drug-addicted prostitute. She knew that her destructive lifestyle was killing her, but she couldn't deal with the feelings that emerged when she was sober. For years she chose to suppress her feelings of hopelessness, guilt, and regret. She never realized the impact that abortion would have on her life and future.

> Even while we're thinking maybe nothing will ever change, forces are at work that we simply cannot see.

There is a powerful principle to hang onto in circumstances that seem hopeless. Even while we're thinking, *Maybe nothing will ever change,* forces are at work that we simply cannot see. We never know what is waiting for us around the corner, next week, or in the next sixty minutes! St. Peter slaved away on his father's fishing boat his entire life, never imagining anything different for himself and his family. It was the only life his family had known for generations. In a single morning, after one encounter with Jesus of Nazareth, suddenly he, a common fisherman, was thrust into the inner circle of the most influential rabbi of his time. He witnessed and participated in numerous miraculous events, including walking on water, and was closely mentored by Jesus Christ himself. Eventually, even after catastrophic failure as a disciple, he was restored and went on to powerfully lead a movement that has to this day never lost momentum. His life changed forever, and the world changed because of him. Bet he never saw that coming!

Remember Susan Boyle from *Britain's Got Talent*? Susan was the youngest of nine children, tucked away in a small village in Scotland. Bullied as a child for being "simple," she never ventured beyond living with her parents, a miner and a shorthand typist. Her beautiful voice won her a small competition here and there, but it never amounted to much. That is, until

April 11, 2009, when Susan Boyle, awkward, forty-eight years old and never been kissed, brought the world to their knees with her breathtaking rendition of "I Dreamed a Dream." In a single day, tens of millions of people adored her, launching a globe-trotting career.

Bernie Nathanson trudged along for ten slow years, day after day. Although he felt hopeless, unseen forces had surrounded him with a massive community of faith, many of whom prayed for his soul. He was well aware of this and moved by their compassion for him, but he was unable to internalize it. He did not believe in God and could not imagine his mind ever changing. His self-worth was dwindling, his value was dissipating—he felt like a throwaway, which seemed to validate his suicidal thoughts. It's not that he was unwilling to believe; Bernie simply could not swallow belief without reason. He was an intellectual to the core; and just like his "conversion" from pro-abortion to anti-abortion, he could not pretend to embrace what had not penetrated the darkness of his desperate quest. But, when he was with the pro-life community, most of whom were Christians, he did feel something intangible and familiar. It was that same atmosphere he experienced back in medical school when in the presence of his beloved professor, Karl Stern. It was peace.

When Bernie Nathanson dragged himself out of bed on a bitterly cold morning in 1989, he had no way of knowing he was about to encounter another profound, life-altering, defining moment. At Second Avenue and Twenty-First Street in New York City, he joined 1,200 participants of Operation Rescue for a peaceful demonstration in front of a Planned Parenthood clinic. His interest in this particular sit-in was to interview participants, gathering information for an article he planned to publish in an ethics journal. The article researched the moral and ethical aspects of these types of demonstrations.

He studied their faces, interviewed various demonstrators, and wrote copious notes while circulating among them. Joining hands and swaying, the demonstrators sang hymns softly, with "pure love on their faces."[2] Equal numbers of Catholics and Protestants together prayed for the unborn babies, for the abortion doctors and nurses, for the confused and frightened pregnant women. They even prayed for the protestors who hurled vile insults at them, the unsympathetic media, and the police officers assigned to the demonstration. They prayed for each other, but never for themselves. In his view, they were simply confident in the rightness of their cause and were persuaded that love would triumph. They sacrificed their time, money, and even freedom for the tiny babies who were unable to thank them.

As the atmosphere penetrated his consciousness, something shifted deep in Bernie's aching soul. His spiritual DNA, which had been repressed since childhood, began to awaken. His mind, will, and emotions had so dominated his life that any spiritual awareness was silenced. But in that moment something in him began to seriously question what Force would enable them to do this. What Force had placed him there at this exact time and place? For the first time in his adult life, Bernie began to honestly consider the reality of God. He simultaneously felt convicted of his arrogant high crimes against others and comprehended a sliver of hope "in the growing belief that someone had died for my sins and my evil two thousand years ago."[3]

One of the amazing things about God is that when we are ready, He has already put a network in place to move us through our circumstances and right into our destiny. This was true for Lisa and Kathy, and this was certainly the case for Bernie Nathanson. In 1986, due to their mutual love of great literature, he had made the acquaintance with Opus Dei priest, Father John McCloskey. Opus Dei is an order of the Catholic

Church that is dedicated to encouraging lay people to aspire to sanctity without changing their state of life or occupation. Father McCloskey, who operated out of Washington's Catholic Information Center a couple of blocks from the White House, earned the nickname "The Spiritual K Street Lobbyist" because of his effective work with powerful members of numerous think tanks, lobbyists, and advocacy groups. Before becoming a priest he had worked on Wall Street at Citibank and Merrill Lynch for a number of years. A gifted intellect, McCloskey was and is passionate about helping influential individuals find their way to God. In recent years he guided and converted Newt Gingrich and Sam Brownback, to name a few.

A quick fix to the immense burden of guilt had never been his goal.

Bernie would drop by Father McCloskey's office often and stay for hours discussing spiritual matters among other things with the well-read priest. McCloskey would periodically hand him great writings that offered actual solutions to the problem of sin. Thus, literature of conversion replaced the literature of sin on Bernie's nightstand. Books by Malcolm Muggeridge, C. S. Lewis, and Cardinal Newman. Like a voice out of his past, Bernie reconnected with his beloved professor Karl Stern. Stern's own book *Pillar of Fire* filled his mind and heart with rich light for the new perspective expanding in his reviving spirit. McCloskey was more than capable of matching Nathanson intellectually.

Conversion did not happen overnight. Over a period of seven years Bernie studied, reasoned, pondered, and digested the reality of his Creator and the implications for him personally. A quick fix to the immense burden of guilt had never been his goal. He longed for and knew he must have real, substantial absolution.

We are all wired uniquely. For some, the light of Truth breaks through because of an emotional experience, which is then bolstered by intellectual understanding. Others encounter a blend of the two. For Bernie Nathanson, nothing would move him but intellectual understanding steering a genuine heart shift. Both were satisfied beyond his imagining. In December 1996, he was baptized a Catholic by Cardinal John O'Connor at New York's St. Patrick's Cathedral and received confirmation and first communion. In his words on the experience, "I was in a real whirlpool of emotion, and then there was this healing, cooling water on me, and soft voices, and an inexpressible sense of peace. I had found a safe place."[4]

A deep work, which had begun in Bernie's mind, made the so-called twelve-inch journey to his heart and eventually brought healing to his spirit. A close friend, Deacon Fournier, quoted Josemaría Escrivá in observing, "Some men, like fish, need to be caught by their head.' Bernie was such a man."

19

LISA

Putting the Train Back on Track

"No matter what your situation,
remind yourself you still have a choice."

~Deepak Chopra

God saved my life through a Twelve Step recovery program. Not only did He save my life, but His grace infiltrated my heart. There are few places on the planet where you will find the level of acceptance, love, and honesty as in the rooms of recovery. My first introduction to substance abuse recovery meetings was in the '80s, and it took me ten years to make it back. *This type of recovery isn't for me. It is for weak, hopeless people.* That was what I thought until I became desperate for change, until I truly wanted the insanity to stop. Finally, somehow I came to a major realization: I was responsible for my own life. Truly, I was sick and tired of being sick and tired. I didn't really know how or if this recovery thing would work, but I didn't have a clue about any other solution.

In 1990 I started attending Twelve Step meetings on a regular basis and practicing the principles of "the program" one day at a time—principals like honesty, open-mindedness, and willingness. Besides desperation, the attraction to Twelve Step recovery was some strange sense of solace, something I knew nothing about but sensed there. I was always told that the only place you find real peace is with God, and in my mind that meant organized religion. But this didn't feel religious, confining, or legalistic. God reveals Himself anywhere that love abounds, weaving His transforming light into our formerly dark existence. God's light finally broke through to Bernie on that sidewalk surrounded by pro-life protesters filled with unconditional love. Trust me, the last place you were going to find me was in a church. It wasn't because I didn't want God, but I thought God didn't want me. Plus, there was nothing that any church had that I wanted! It was full of self-righteous, holier-than-thou people who had not a clue about my life, nor did they care. At least that is what I thought.

One thing I didn't count on was that not only God, but Jesus Christ lived in the rooms of recovery. Most of the groups' ideas are not original or new; they were first introduced in the sayings and principles of Jesus. Let's take the concept of anonymity. It is a foundation of Twelve Step recovery. That's partly because many members naturally do not want their affiliation with a recovery group known. But anonymity also ensures that no one person could take credit for a mutual undertaking. Just like Jesus taught as recorded in the gospel of Matthew, "Give your gifts in private, and your Father, who sees everything, will reward you" (Matt. 6:4 NLT).

There are no leaders in Twelve Step programs, just servants. In a world full of power struggles, Twelve Step philosophy has remained unique in its ability to limit individual power. This concept is in direct correlation to what the Jesus told His disciples: "Whosoever will be chief among you, let him be your servant" (Matt. 20:27 KJV).

Jesus is no respecter of people, but neither are alcohol and drugs—they are equal opportunity employers. Matthew again recorded Jesus saying, "But I say to you, love your enemies and pray for those who persecute you . . . For if you love those who love you, what reward do you have?" (Matt. 5:44–46 NASB). This is an example of the all-inclusive love of Christ. This type of love is a beacon of hope that shines so brightly to people who, like me, were considered disposable and life's throwaways. People in Twelve Step recovery have learned how to rise above their feelings and love all people, putting principles above personalities. This is what Jesus is all about.

> God reveals Himself anywhere that love abounds.

I was beginning to understand and know my God—none other than Jesus Christ himself!

At first I used the meetings for a social outlet and assistance with my drug addiction, which brought me a measure of comfort. Recovery meetings helped me gain perspective on myself. I guess you could say I was gaining some sort of humility, as well as the courage to live life on life's terms. In order for any regeneration to work, I had to be willing to surrender to its process—throw in the towel and remain teachable. After all, my best thinking got me here.

Although I attended meetings several times a week I still was drinking occasionally. In the beginning I took public transportation to get to meetings, but people in recovery are always willing to help. Many times I caught a ride to meetings or other recovery functions with one of my newfound friends. Working for a temp agency allowed for really good, high-paying assignments; and this enabled me to buy a car and begin to save a little money. This of course was in 1990 and the Internet was fairly new, so again background checks weren't prevalent; in fact they were non-existent unless you needed a security clearance. Landing a long-term, six-month secretarial assignment gave me a bit of security, but I knew it all depended on whether I could stay away from the crack pipe.

At the time I was living with my boyfriend, who had actually been my court-appointed attorney who tried my forgery case when I was incarcerated. He showed up one night, out of the blue, at the Italian restaurant where I was working. He asked me out, and of course I said yes. Within a few weeks I moved in with him and was thrilled at the prospect. But sometimes things that seem like good ideas turn out not to be. I had great gratitude toward Dane for providing a beautiful place to live and some semblance of consistency, but it was all still a game. The place and players were different, perhaps of higher economic standing, but my feelings about myself were heading back to that infamous childhood bridge. As long as I did as I was told to do, then I was loved. But the moment my actions didn't line up with Dane's expectations all that love disappeared. I was nothing more than a high-class call girl—which provided him the justification to secretly see other women. So I figured what's good for the gander is good for the goose!

I spotted an attractive guy who worked in my section. He had a friendly smile, and we began chatting a little every morning. At first he was just another handsome man, but that changed. There was just something different about this guy, how he looked at me and answered my questions. I was used to having men pay attention to me, but this was interest. He valued my opinions and observations, treating me with respect, as an equal. He made me feel important, worth investing time in. This opened the door for me to even ask his advice about my dysfunctional relationship and living situation. You see, the best way I knew to get out of one relationship was just to get into another. Persistently I dropped hints, hoping he would ask me out, but he didn't. We went to lunch a few times, but it never progressed into anything more. So finally I just couldn't stand it another minute and I blurted out, "Do you want to go out this weekend?"

His response totally took me by surprise. "No, Lisa, I don't make a habit of dating women who are living with another man."

Surely I must have misheard him. "What, you're kidding, right?"

"No, you heard me right. But hey, if things change, let me know, and then I would love to take you out."

By this time steam was coming out my ears! I was used to getting my way with men. At the same time I was absolutely amazed; you could have knocked me over with a feather. Never had I met a man with such conviction, with those types of standards. Here was a man that I couldn't manipulate. In fact, I had never met a man who didn't want to date me.

When someone told me no I translated that to mean there must be another way. Always ready for a challenge, I wanted to further investigate. *What was this guy all about?* Because I was making fairly good money, I was finally able to leave the man I was living with and move into a room being rented out by a coworker.

As soon as I brought the last box from my car into my new residence, I gave Tom a call; and, true to his word, he asked me out to dinner. It was late September 1990. We met at a popular bar and then went for a quiet Chinese meal. The date was so nice—actually getting to know him and being treated so well. Given the condition of my mind and past experience, I assumed that our first date would end the next morning. We talked about so much and had gotten around to the topic of music when I turned on my special brand of charm: "So, what kind of music do you like to make love to?" He just about choked on his General Tso's chicken. His face beet red, he replied, "I am forty-three and have been divorced for ten years, and at this stage in my life a fly-by-night relationship is of no interest to me."

I was astounded and amazed. *I just have to get to know this guy and find out what makes him tick.* The fact that he was a moral, decent guy never crossed my mind. I wonder why? All I could think was, *What the heck is happening here?* This was unfamiliar territory to me, especially in light of the low-quality men who had passed through my life over the previous fifteen years.

Justification was the name of my game.

After dating only a short time, I was pushing to move in together. I wore him down by continually justifying why we should cohabitate. After all, justification was the name of my game. I could validate and rationalize anything if I worked hard at it. Tom conceded and made a place for my clothes in the closet and my face cream on the bathroom vanity. During this time I continued with my recovery meetings but was still having an occasional drink. For those of you reading this and struggling with addiction and think this may be an option for you, I would advise against it. It will get you into trouble. Recovery means total abstinence from all mood-altering substances!

One evening after I drank two vodka and tonics, Tom very carefully asked, "Why do you go to recovery meetings and still drink?"

Justifiably, I explained, "I go to meetings so I won't use drugs. Alcohol was never really my problem. Drugs were the problem that just about killed me."

The following Friday we met a few of his friends for happy hour. And let me tell you, his friends were entirely different from the type of "friends" I had been associating with for the past few years. These people actually owned homes, had jobs, a car, and families. Needless to say, I was a bit uncomfortable. With each drink though, I fit in better, feeling as though I belonged, wittier and charmingly likeable. For the three beers Tom drank over the two-hour stretch, I drank twelve "rusty nail" cocktails. You might guess this brought me to the porcelain throne for most of the night. The next day I swore off liquor forever!

We had plans to go away the following weekend. My temporary job had ended, and I was hired on full-time with a commercial realty company. Leaving for work that Friday morning, I said, "Have a good day. See you right after work. It's payday, so I am going to stop by the bank and be home by 5:30." We kissed and said good-bye. Those were my plans, and I fully intended on following through. People let me tell you, the mind of an addict is a heart-breaking riddle. For all intents and purposes, my life was getting better. But this unexpected love from this new man was creating a fear deep inside me; it was a fear that I would never really be able to fully enjoy a good and normal life. My mind was like a movie screen playing before me all my sins. All of those degrading things that I had done came flooding back. Full of guilt and shame, I couldn't take it. I had to find relief. Instead of going directly to the bank, I decided to have a drink after work with a former acquaintance. But remember, "One is too many, and a thousand are never enough!" Before I knew it, I was paying a visit to my old familiar stomping grounds, landing at my favorite crack house.

Tremendously familiar with the consequences I would endure for this poor choice about to be made, not to mention the lingering pain and remorse it would cause, I did it anyway. Having one moment of clarity before I got high, I remembered the red-lipped officer's words, "You are not the type of woman who belongs in jail." Pushing that thought as far out of my mind as possible, I put the pipe to my mouth and inhaled deeply. I just couldn't get high enough to take away the all too familiar feeling of defeat. Every time my high started to wear off, reality came rushing in like a bone-crushing juggernaut of pain.

By Sunday morning, I had lost everything good and positive that had been gained over the past nine months: my bender that weekend cost me my paycheck, my savings account, my jewelry, and, worst of all, my dignity. I was totally bankrupt—physically, emotionally, mentally, and spiritually. I just wanted the pain to stop. But the worst was yet to come. I had to make the call, the dreaded call that I knew would end yet another relationship—the best I had ever had. I had destroyed another home, and this would leave me to my own sick demise.

Tom answered immediately, "Are you all right?"

I was absolutely exhausted after being up for forty-eight hours straight. "No, I am not all right. I got high, and I need you to come and get me."

"Tell me where you are, and I will be right there."

Minutes later, he pulled up in his black Chevy Blazer. He reached across and swung the door open, "Get in."

I held my breath thinking, *This is it. Same stuff, different day. Brace yourself for the barrage of obscenities and degrading remarks that will be thrown your way.* I got into the car in the same dress that I had worn to work on Friday morning.

Without hesitation he put his arms around me and said, "Lisa, why do you keep doing this to yourself? What can I do to help you? I love you, and I don't want you to live like this."

Tears rushed down my face. Confusion filled my mind. Suddenly a total shift in the atmosphere took place. *What did he just say?* Never in all my life did anyone ever ask if they could help me, never. Usually it was, "What is wrong with you?" or "You are a crack-head whore! Pack your stuff and get out."

When someone did offer assistance there was always an ulterior motive—a price to be paid, robbing me of my value and esteem.

Although you may not have experienced my type of circumstances, you might well relate to my feelings of rejection and abandonment. You know what I mean by the "you will never amount to anything" comments or the horrible feeling of another botched relationship. How about the depression and oppression of just surviving and barely getting by?

Because of Tom's healing words of love and compassion, I was able to embrace hope. Hope produces faith. When this man showed up on that precise morning, it was no ordinary liberation. It was a sacred rescue or a divine appointment, and those can only be engineered by God Himself. An awakening occurred deep in my spirit. There had to be a God for me to be able to feel this type of mercy. Could this possibly be the God that was spoken of in the rooms of recovery? Could there really be this Higher Power who loved me so unconditionally that he sent this man to express to me my true value? Through the power of love, my whole world changed that Sunday morning. It was April 5, 1991.

Change I must or die I will. That day is when I began the long, painful, and ongoing process of letting go. I had to do something different if I wanted the life I saw in so many people in the rooms of recovery. Through the course of working the Twelve Steps you uncover underlying issues you weren't even aware of. "Issues" are really just a nice way of describing sin. I learned that the consequences of sin are much worse than its intent. You can never predict the torrent of havoc it will unleash on your life.

I also realized that I was living in a fantasy land of lawlessness, with no one to hold me accountable for my actions.

Change I must
or die I will.

But deep inside, I longed for someone to tell me that the way I was living my life was wrong! Not only that it was wrong, but how it could be fixed. *Please somebody, fix me!* I tried to detach myself from personal consequences, but I couldn't. I wanted a magic solution—one to extinguish the torment of my own actions and poor decisions that ached deep within my soul. Even though I may have spent a large majority of my life in a drunken, drug-induced stupor, some memories cannot be erased. They must be forgiven.

Jesus said, "If you seek you will find." The operative word here is *if.* Some of us will not seek until we have worn out every other option known to man. That was me—but now I was finally desperate for change. Even though I had rejected Him so many times, God never stopped pursuing me. Tom was sent that morning to show me God's unconditional love and unmerited grace. That divine appointment would prepare me for one of the most important decisions in my life, one that would realign my destiny. But just like most things in my life, I could have never guessed how it would unfold.

In the "program," after the official end to the hour-long group recovery meeting, we always say, "Stay around for the meeting after the meeting." Basically it was an invitation to hang out and get to know people on a more personal basis. While I was chatting it up with a girlfriend, an older gentleman approached me with a handful of cassette tapes bundled by a rubber band. He told me that he had been watching me for a while and that I had that "star" quality. When he saw that in a person, his goal was to magnify and bring that quality into the light. Of course, given my past experience I immediately wondered, *What is this old man up to? What does he really want?* He then handed me the bundle of tapes and told me to make sure to take time and listen to them. The tapes were entitled "Grace, Grace and More Grace." So I headed to my car and popped one of the tapes into my cassette player. When I heard the voice of the person on the tape I could not even determine if it was a really feminine man or an extremely masculine woman. So immediately, with contempt prior to investigation, I ejected the tape, tossed it on the floor of the passenger seat, and did not give it another thought.

The next day on my way to the meeting I saw the tape that I had tossed on the floor and something kept telling me to give it another try. This time the sound I heard was different. It was a woman whose voice brought me an overwhelming sense of love. She was a popular radio evangelist. I couldn't really tell you what was on those tapes because all I heard was this: no matter what you have done, no matter the gravity of your shame and acuteness of your pain there is help, real help and that help is JESUS. He can wash away your past, give you a clean heart and fresh start.

Sometimes we just have to be in the right environment, in the right place at the right time, and miracles will happen. Pulling the car off the road onto the shoulder I looked up like I had many times before, but this time I was ready. "Lord, if you are really there, save me! Help me! I have tried to do things my own way for years, and look where it has gotten me. I know I have sinned—please forgive me." That day in my car, I could feel the love of Jesus and responded to His invitation to accept Him into my heart, surrendering to Him total control as my Lord and Savior. For years I knew who Jesus was, but I didn't know Him. All I knew was religion. That day he showed me the depths of my sin and the depths of His heart of mercy and grace for me.

Up to this point my impression of God and His love was based on performance—what you did, not who you were. Before long, I began to realize that my identity was in Him and that it was good; because He created me, and God doesn't make junk!

For years I had tried to gain identity in other ways: through lies, through sexuality, through escapism, and even through Markus. But it was in God that I found my true identity—the original DNA that had been deposited in my spirit while being knit together in my mother's womb. In meetings I could feel Him wrap His arms around me. When people would take the podium and tell their story of redemption something happened to me that helped me to understand His love and redemption for all who sought Him. The direction of my thinking began to change. Slowly I began to realize I was significant, which I had never felt before in my entire life. This newfound purpose and realization motivated me and created hope for my future. This was a security and peace that I wanted more of.

> Happiness is a byproduct of right living.

This was only the beginning of this new life! That same year on the Fourth of July weekend, Tom and I had planned a trip to the beach to visit my parents. My parents got up early and headed out, so we were alone. The same man, who just months prior had picked me up at the crack house and had seen me at my lowest point, got down on his knee and asked me to marry him. For years I had felt like nothing more than discarded trash. Never in my wildest dreams did I think I was worthy of this kind of love, but with God all things are possible. On September 29, 1991, a beautiful, clear autumn day, we said our vows and started our new life together as Mr. and Mrs. Joseph (Tom) Thomas.

My husband's kindness and compassion was and still is a gift from God. I needed a man who had the patience to let me grow and allow God to purge all the trash from my life, who would love me in spite of my growing pains. It takes a strong man who knows his own worth to embrace this. He saw in me what I could not see in myself. His love for me has helped me grasp the fullness of the grace of God. Tom helped me find my purpose and genuinely begin to live life, not just exist.

Did you know that you can actually choose to be joyful and grateful? And that happiness is a byproduct of right living? I sure didn't, but I was beginning to explore the possibility. Grounded in recovery and the Word of God, I began to see seeds of hope sprout right before my eyes. My entire life was turning around. Part of me was satisfied with this level of renewal. I was not where I wanted to be, but I was far better than I was before. However, there was still a lingering, uncomfortable uneasiness deep inside that I needed to resolve. The Bible says that we will be transformed by the renewing of our mind. It isn't an event; it is an ongoing pursuit.

I knew I was making great strides, but there was something I had not addressed. There was yet something hidden that was keeping me from walking in freedom. Fear kept me from moving forward, and resisting help only prolonged the pain. This is when I realized that for me to continue to progress, I would have to begin healing the "inner" me, digging down in the depths of my soul and unearthing the pain, hurt, and shame that I had buried in the depth of my being.

This was a lesson I would soon fully embrace.

20

KATHY
The Fruit of Failure

"The good news of suffering is that
it brings us to the end of ourselves—
a purpose it has certainly served in my life.
It brings us to the place of honesty, which is
the place of desperation, which is the place of faith,
which is the place of freedom."

~TULLIAN TCHIVIDJIAN

Dave and I found a beautiful house in the suburbs of Virginia, only forty-five minutes from the nation's capital. Shortly after we moved, our third son was born. Yes, this was just the fresh start we needed. Our neighborhood was new and thriving, complete with walking paths and a community pool. The landscape was beautiful, and I spent hours outside with our boys and quickly got to know our neighbors. And just down the street was Lisa Kratz Thomas, a beautiful woman brimming with energy and a refreshingly unique approach to life. The neighborhood was filled with young, successful, happy families. Correction: *perfect* families. Families who had it all figured out. Or so I thought.

Having left family behind in Colorado still in sharp disagreement with us, I became more determined than ever to prove myself. They doubted my perspective, and I felt like I'd lost my credibility and value. *After all, I was the victim here! Why couldn't they see that?* It didn't matter; I didn't need them anyway. I would just have to demonstrate that I was in the right by excelling in my life. Perfectionism kicked back into high gear as a way to feel OK about myself without the support system I had relied on in the past.

Relying on my strength, the one thing I knew I was good at, I decided to host a weekly ladies group. I'd done this many times before and confidently invited everyone in the neighborhood to a Bible study in my home. The morning of the first meeting women came pouring in and filled the living room. When Lisa walked through my front door something in the atmosphere altered; it was electrified. I was immediately struck by her beauty, humor, and confidence. Fashionable and vivacious, her presence announced, "Look out, world, here I come!" She wasn't afraid to speak her mind, and her questions and comments were insightful. She was easily the energy and glue that held the group together. I thought, *Now this is a woman I want to get to know!* In spite of all that could be intimidating about her, she had a way of putting me at ease. A rare combination.

A few weeks into our meetings, Lisa stayed after and we chatted at my kitchen table over coffee. By now I knew that she came from a background of drug abuse and had been sober for three years. It was clear to me that she possessed an unmistakable spiritual stability. This was a woman who knew how to take spiritual truths and put them into action where the rubber meets the road. And then she told me the rest of her story.

I couldn't believe it. How in the world could this vibrant woman have lived through such unspeakable heartache?

Gorgeous, put-together Lisa strung out on drugs and pimped out on the streets of DC? She had suffered destitution and domestic violence at a level I couldn't even imagine. My own troubles lessened in the light of what she had endured. My respect for her catapulted into a new stratosphere as I took in the transformation in her life. I began to open up to her about the chaos of my life, broken relationships, and hurts from my past. She didn't even bat an eyelash. Nothing surprised or shocked her. She took it all in with grace and intuitive comprehension. And then she reflected on the vulnerable personal story I shared. Her conversation was seasoned with solid, simplistic truths, and with hope. I didn't have even an inkling of how desperately I would need her only a few months later.

Dave's job was going well, and I was quickly weaving into the fabric of this new community. But underneath the surface all was not going well. I tormented myself with thoughts of self-doubt. Everyone around me seemed so dang confident.

Their houses are spotless and decorated beautifully. You can't even keep the toys picked up and the dishes clean. All these stay-at-home moms in the neighborhood are just taking a break from their successful careers. All you have is a bachelor's degree, and you aren't even using it. They all have plenty of money, and we can't even afford a babysitter.

The pace of life was breakneck. Expectations for achievement were high. One of the moms of a preschooler casually told me, "I took my daughter to the Matisse collection in DC, and she loved it." *What in the heck is Matisse? Or is it a 'who'? Is that some sort of papier-mâché art form?* I was planning to homeschool our three boys; I'd better learn about "Matisse," whatever it was, quickly. Remember, I absolutely had to be the ultimate mom. It was the key to my world being OK.

Within a few months we found ourselves in over our heads financially. The cost of living was way higher than we'd anticipated. Many weeks my husband was gone, traveling for business, and I was holding down the fort with three small children. Everywhere I turned people seemed to have it together. Destructive emotions of jealousy and insecurity cropped up on a daily basis, producing deep frustration. *If only we made more money I could buy nice furniture and feel better about my house. We could get the fancy van with the wood side panels.* (Yes, that was considered fancy once!) *We could spend glamorous evenings in DC and take advantage of the sophisticated urban culture. Why doesn't anyone else have to deal with the crap I'm dealing with? None of them have to get help with recovering from childhood sexual abuse.*

> Destructive emotions of jealousy and insecurity cropped up on a daily basis.

Even though I felt jealous, I also felt superior. I was convinced that we knew the secrets of raising children with my religious and academic background. *I can't believe none of these women are going to homeschool their children! How can they be so smart and not know about homeopathy and the value of homemade whole wheat bread? Why aren't their kids in Sunday school and memorizing Bible verses?*

All the while, I was sagging under the weight of the disappointment of falling out with my extended family. My feelings were conflicted. Although I was extremely lonely and missing my family tremendously, stubbornly my heart remained indignant and angry. Back then I didn't know the enormous weight resentment loaded onto the person who refused to let go. I also didn't know how dangerous it was.

One sunny August morning, worn out, house poor, and feeling incurably inadequate, I broke—mentally, emotionally, and physically. Walking away from the desk after going through all the unpaid bills, my body started shaking and a roaring sound filled my ears. My skin burned and prickled. *Why is the room spinning? Oh my God, I'm having a panic attack! Oh my God, this can't be happening. Oh my God, help! Help! This can't be happening!*

I cannot describe the intensity of my terror over the next three or four days. Unlike the panic attacks years ago, this one wasn't going away. It was relentless—hour after hour, day after day, with only brief periods of relief. Those who have experienced this before know it literally feels like you are going to die. My husband was freaking out, never having seen me like this before. What happened to the woman he'd married?

My own thoughts were no less tortured. *I have got to end this. I'm going to have to kill myself,* kept racing through my mind. Then I'd look at the boys and Dave. I knew I couldn't do that to them. Besides, my family had already lost my brother; I couldn't put them through that again. I was trapped. I would never feel normal again—I'd just have to gut it out in miserable agony for the rest of my life.

We called my in-laws to tell them we were in serious crisis and needed help with the boys. My mother-in-law was on a plane to Virginia the next day. I was so embarrassed by my inability to function. Panic attacks as a kid were humiliating enough, but this was over the top. I was a full-grown woman and couldn't hide my fear. But I was desperate, and what a godsend she was!

Somehow we survived, and a few days later we were sitting in the office with the head of psychiatry at a major Washington, DC, clinic. He happened to be a friend of the family and had worked us in as his first appointment for the day. (Talk about God helping you when you can't help yourself!) Before we even had a chance to explain our crisis, he started by calmly describing exactly what I was feeling emotionally and physically.

"Feels like you're going to die, right? Like you're standing in line at the grocery store and turn around to find a Bengal tiger chasing you? Feels like it will never stop?"

I nodded in surprise. How in the world did he know this? I didn't know anyone who had ever felt like I did.

"You're clinically depressed. Some medication will calm you down enough so you can get some therapy to work on the root issues."

Wait a minute. Did I hear him right? Depressed? I was *terrified*, not a little blue! He recommended hospitalization, but my fear of abandonment was back in full force, and there was no way I was letting my family out of my sight. We left with the doctor assuring us that it wouldn't last long with the right treatment. Oh, how I needed to hear that—just the promise of light at the end of the tunnel can help you hang on another day. I felt like Bernie, putting off his suicide one day at a time in the slim hope that tomorrow just might be better. Tomorrow I might find the right combination to escape my suffering and be able to truly live.

The following weeks felt like forever as I waited out the panic attacks and wasted away to ninety-five pounds, too anxiety-ridden to stomach food. I gave up on my ideals of home schooling and enrolled our oldest at the local elementary school. A neighbor who taught an innovative preschool in her home knocked on my door asking if our second son would be interested in joining. I told her, "I would love for him to, but we just don't have the money for it. I'm so sorry." A few days later she showed up on my doorstep again and said, "I'd like to include him anyway. Free of charge." This was the last thing I expected. I responded, "That would be awesome, but I don't have any way to repay you." She waved me off and replied, "Don't worry about it. I'm sure I'll think of something." There was nothing I thought I had to offer, but I said OK and thanked her anyway.

The psychiatrist had told me that morning walks and sunshine would help with depression, and again I thought, "Let's be real here—this is *panic!*" But I obeyed. It was on a bright sunny morning, as I was shuffling around the block, that I found myself ringing Lisa's doorbell. The door swung open, Lisa took one look at me and grabbed my hand and led me to a sitting room. She didn't look the least bit worried as I described my pitiful state. In fact, she was the only person other than the doctor who wasn't intimidated by my breakdown.

I had to go back to foundational truths before I could embrace what would save me from my torment.

She looked me in the eyes and said, "Kathy, you're going to be fine! Don't you know Jesus loves you? If you were the only person alive, He still would have died just to save you! All you have to do is just Let Go, and Let God."

All I could do was stare at her thinking, *Clichés? Are you kidding me? I needed deep spiritual answers to solve my monumental problems! Do you know who you're talking to? Don't you know how complex I am? My life is much more serious than Sunday school answers!* But there is a difference between clichés and simple truth. I had no comprehension then that I was being handed pure gold from a black belt in Twelve Step recovery. These weren't any lightweight platitudes; they were solid tools for building a sturdy foundation for life. I might not have been able to take in her words, but I did see the love and light in her eyes. I held on for dear life.

My excruciating pain brought to the surface a fundamental question I had no idea needed answering in my life. *Is God real? If He is, is He enough to help me survive and eventually bring joy back to my life?* I had to go back to foundational truths before I could embrace what Lisa promised would save me from my torment. My reasoning went something like this: Jesus Christ was a historical figure, not a figment of someone's imagination. He said He was God. Either He lied, He was delusional, or He was right. Hundreds of people witnessed His death, and hundreds more saw Him resurrected. Because that was true, I could believe what He demonstrated and said about the nature of God. With him nothing is impossible. When that reasoning settled in my heart it stuck, and I never turned back. And I did get better. The moment I believed, the darkness of fear was pushed aside and God illuminated my soul.

Once I got relief from the acute panic, I started counseling with a skilled therapist. But I still saw my crisis as being caused by outside circumstances. I still thought others were to blame. I wasn't able to see that the root issue, a cycle of comparison and perfectionism, was the culprit in my horrible ordeal. Less than two years later, following the birth of our fourth son, I found myself right back in the throes of another nervous breakdown. Let me tell you—that was humbling. Have you ever heard of looking for the common denominator in all of your problems and then finding out that it's you?

This time, I put my grievances aside and got on the phone and called my own mother. Through tears I managed to choke out, "Mom, I'm in trouble and I need your help." Without hesitating she graciously said yes and flew out the next day to help us with the kids. Coming to the end of myself for the second time, I was done blaming anyone else. Her help in my crisis began some much-needed healing in our relationship.

And Lisa was right there again, holding my hand and telling me those same confident words of love and hope. I still didn't comprehend how "Let go and let God" was supposed to pull me out of what I saw as insurmountable, life-threatening problems. But I borrowed her faith until I could hang on to my own. How I needed that confidence!

As the painful days inched by, I was astounded to realize that I had a deep anger toward God and I was demanding answers. *God, how dare you! You never asked my permission to put me on this earth with all this pain and uncertainty!* I realized I was actually thinking, *I wish I'd never taken that first breath. Maybe it would have been better if the doctor hadn't revived me in the delivery room.* Here I thought I had been so surrendered to God all my life. But I had a decision to make: was I going to trust Him to be in charge, or was I going to stay defiant? Either God was everything, or He was nothing. My answer was yes, I believed He knew what He was doing and I needed to surrender and align my will with His. Peace settled over me. Through obedience, the shadows were pushed aside and I began to live out my light-filled destiny ignited by the fire of fresh revelation.

You see, I was so angry and so bent on trying to make things work in my life, I didn't even realize I had a deep wound that needed to be healed before I could be restored. Some wounds are hidden, buried so deeply we don't even know they exist. I had rearranged my circumstances and tried to force people to do what I thought they needed to do. I was putting a Band-Aid on my surface symptoms. All the while, God saw my wounds— wounds hidden in the darkness that I had denied or forgot even existed. And He loves us too much to let us keep pushing forward in self-destructive ways. Our pain serves a vital purpose, urging us to look to a higher wisdom.

Did you know that humbling ourselves and needing help from others can truly offer us gifts we never would have found otherwise? Remember that neighbor who taught preschool and took in my sweet son? A few months after I'd recovered, she found out that I knew how to play piano. She rang my doorbell again and said, "I figured out how you can pay me back. You can teach my eleven-year-old daughter piano!" I protested that I didn't have a degree in piano performance and had never taught anyone how to play piano and probably wasn't qualified. She pooh-poohed that idea and said she'd bring her daughter over the following week. How could I say no? I went to the local music store and picked out a beginner piano curriculum.

During her first lesson, I was so nervous my hands were shaking and I was stumbling over my own words. But we both made it through, and before I knew it, I had fourteen students and a nice little extra income! All because my need opened a door of opportunity.

Partway into our fifth year in Virginia, my husband accepted a job offer in Dallas, Texas. Piling our four boys into a brand new Astro van (minus the wood paneling), we pulled a loaded U-Haul halfway across the country. Six months later, after having been crammed into a small apartment during the dog days of a hot Texas summer, we moved into our new house in a suburb north of Dallas. And that house just happened to be within jogging distance of a couple we had known since childhood. Mandy, a spunky, cheerful redheaded mother of four grown kids, threw her arm around my shoulder and asked me, "Hey, Kathy, how would you like to go to a Twelve Step meeting with me?"

21

LISA'S
Legacy

"The greatest legacy one can pass on
to one's children and grandchildren is not money
or other material things accumulated in one's life,
but rather a legacy of character, faith and love."

~Billy Graham

God is so caring, compassionate, and wise that He doesn't make us deal with all our sin right away. These things were so painful, they were hidden deep inside. This kind of pain can also survive suppression. There is some trauma that doesn't hit you right away; it takes time. You may not even realize its hold on you until you start healing from other difficulties. This was true in my life. Since the day that I made the decision to turn my life and its care over to Jesus, nothing was the same! A new sense of purpose rose up in me; the recovery meetings that I had attended for social reasons started to become my lifeline.

I had total support from the man who "rocked my world" by accepting me just as I was, but loving me enough not to let me stay that way. Did we live happily ever after? True relationship is more than a fairytale. It takes commitment to a lifelong promise of respect, honesty, and communication. I was not capable of fixing my own life—been there, done that, got the T-shirt. The problem maker could not be the problem solver; the old me needed to give way to new living that would demand rigorous honesty. All of this sounds great in theory, but you may be asking, "How in the world do you do this?"

Getting a mentor was my first move in letting go of my old way of doing things and starting something new. To truly change my warped way of thinking, I had to be willing to listen to suggestions and follow directions. A mentor is affectionately known as a sponsor in Twelve Step recovery. They share their experience, strength, and hope to help newcomers adapt to the program, and boy did I need help! I needed guidance from someone who had made progress in transitioning from a life of drinking and drugging to sobriety. Discipleship from a person who had cultivated a relationship with Jesus and was living it was a must; I needed someone who was willing to call me on my bull and set me straight. For me to even consider submitting to this was a miracle! My philosophy about advice in any form was act first, seek guidance later.

It was recommended that I attend a recovery meeting every day. To start each day in quiet reflection, reading God's Word, praying, and listening for the answers. I was told to get out of my head (my thoughts, fears, and needs) and help someone else. Finally, I needed to check in daily with my sponsor. This started me on the road to working the Twelve Steps.

What does working the steps actually mean? In a nutshell, the steps are a set of spiritual principles designed to clean house and move us closer to God. It is an inner work: admittance of a dependency, recognition and identification of a Higher power, and surrender to that power. Through the Twelve Steps you discover your part and the roots of your dependency and surrender it to God. It is a process of continually asking God to remove your shortcomings and defects, making amends to those you have hurt, and taking daily inventory and promptly admitting your faults. It also includes continuing to pray and meditate on God's will for your life, so you can be helpful and useful to others.

Emerging from the pit of hell, with my feet set on solid ground, I began to feel pretty optimistic, like maybe I could be happy. For years I was always waiting for the other shoe to drop, experiencing violence all around me. Finally I had found peace and I wasn't going to let anything or anybody take that away from me. Eagerly I followed directions because I was finding a new freedom and a new happiness. Soon the compulsion to use, drink, and escape was lifted, and practicing my new lifestyle became exciting and rewarding. Sobriety is a daily reprieve based on my willingness to surrender to spiritual principles. I attended mood-altering meetings instead of using mood-altering substances.

Little by little, the small, simple things in life began to fulfill me, such as taking walks with my husband, watching a good movie, or cooking a great meal. Time with God began to take precedence in my day, filling those empty places inside in a way that I never thought possible. Purpose was erupting, and self-loathing was passing away. Helping others replaced self-seeking. Family restoration was taking place, so gathering for holidays and special occasions became joyful events. Relationships that I had convinced myself didn't matter were brought back to life. Then I began to realize how these bonds helped me connect the dots of my existence. Life was good, which I had not been able to say for a long, long time.

But something was still missing, an emptiness of sorts, a lack of completion and fulfillment. There was a yearning in my soul, overwhelming at times and consuming at best; I wanted to be a mother.

Tom had two children from a previous marriage, and before marriage we had discussed having a child. Although he knew that I'd had multiple abortions, neither he nor I knew the ultimate toll that choice would take on our marriage. I was thirty-one and Tom was forty-four when we got married, so we started trying to conceive immediately. Two years went by without success. Even after all I had gone through during those horrific years of active addiction, these were the longest and most agonizing years of my life. Anytime I would see a baby, a gnawing sense of regret and deep despair would engulf me. Feelings of envy and self-pity reared their ugly head. Have you ever wanted something so bad that it consumed most of your waking hours? There were tests upon tests, procedures and operations.

Have you ever wanted something so bad that it consumed most of your waking hours?

I experienced two opposite but equally untrue reactions. My first inclination was anger: Why me? But that was immediately followed by stinging remorse for the things I had done and the way I had lived my life: Why not me? During the height of my using career, I abandoned the thought and opportunity of being a mother. That decision was now haunting and torturing me beyond belief. Satan vulgarly accused and abused me daily by telling me: "You had your chance. You will never be able to conceive. You were never worthy of motherhood. You murdered your own babies. There are no children left for you."

For the first time, reality about my abortions set in. I had taken the lives of five innocent human beings—five of my own children. Pain over that fact finally began to arise from deep within my soul. Abortion not only takes innocent lives, but it steals our authority as a woman. Abortion is a seductive trick used by the evil one to stop us from fulfilling our purpose in life.

I was designed, predestined to be a mother; and from my initial abortion that hope was taken from me, and it changed me. I believed that I had no value. This is why I so easily accepted being used, beaten up, and thrown out.

When you hear something long enough you begin to believe it. Dr. Nathanson and his cohorts used the same philosophy of repetition in their brilliant marketing campaign to legalize abortion. The more they said it, the more people believed it. The very lie Satan used to entice me, that I would gain freedom through abortion, he was now using as a venomous weapon against me. This only further fostered my low self-worth and added to the confusion in my mind. Sorrow began to fill my heart as I was awakened to the realization that the evil one had been trying to kill me since I was five years old. To ensure that I would be defeated, he utilized the generational pattern of alcoholism to derail my goals and abortion to steal my power.

Having accepted the '70s enlightenment doctrine and falling victim to the radical women's movement, I had been deceived into believing that abortion was my right. Never was I offered any other solution to what I considered to be an unsolvable problem. In fact, everything in my world led me to believe abortion was not only my choice, but the right choice. It was merely a medical procedure. My baby was a clump of tissue, nothing more than a mass of cells. I was never told that at eleven weeks gestation my baby was just over one and a half inches long and almost fully formed. That her hands would soon open and close, that tiny tooth buds would begin to appear under her gums, and some of her bones were beginning to harden and she could feel pain.

My decision to have an abortion was supposed to bring relief and freedom, but it sure felt enslaving to me now. My heart was broken, and I was overcome with grief. Rarely was there a time when I didn't feel underlying anger and rage. I was belligerent and antagonistic, believing all the while I was just born this way. It was my personality. Uncontrollable crying yet emotional numbness were sharply juxtaposed, in large part due to my abortions.

Reflecting on the previous years of alcohol and drug abuse, I had never really connected my addiction and my abortions before now. Would alcohol and drugs have dominated my life the way they had if I hadn't had the abortions? Would I have needed such an obliterating escape strategy if I hadn't created so much chaos to escape from? Today, I know the emotions and feelings I experienced were not only consequences of substance abuse, but symptoms of Post-Abortion Syndrome (PAS), a form of Posttraumatic Stress Disorder, or PTSD. This trauma was so sinister that it morphed itself into the familiar footprint of addiction, thus keeping itself hidden for years. All of this contributed to the enormously vicious cycle of death in which I was engaged.

Above all, my deepest disturbance was the inability to find forgiveness for myself. In previous years, I had been so busy defending abortion that I dismissed any negative feelings of my own. Now, when I would allow my mind to travel back in time to those empty days after the abortions, the anxiety and panic would be so overwhelming I could hardly breathe. I was like a time bomb waiting to go off.

Another month went by, and again I started my period. Not being able to handle these emotions anymore, I went into our bedroom, lay on the floor, and cried out to God. This is what I recall saying to Him that day:

> *Lord, You already know what I have done, and I*
> *can't live like this very much longer. The sin I am guilty of*
> *and the anguish in my heart is unbearable. I know Your*

grace is sufficient for me and You have shown me forgiveness in so many ways. I was hopeless, and You gave me encouragement; I couldn't stop using, and You took away the compulsion; I was promiscuous, and You changed my heart; I was lonely, and You gave me a loving husband. But Father, there is something deep inside me that I have rationalized and hidden for years. I have never even dared to speak of this and have been afraid to ask for Your forgiveness. I have hidden this secret so long, it has encumbered my ability to love You or anyone fully. I have to release this pain to You. Lord, please help me—please forgive me for the five lives I took through abortion. My own children endured the pain of death because of my selfishness. Heal me, help me, and show me how to go on.

I want to be a mother, Lord please!

The *devil* loves nothing more than to drive a wedge between *us* and God; he will stop at nothing. But God says what is intended for harm I shall use for good! After tearfully pleading with the Lord to forgive me and bless me with a child, I felt an urging to pen my emotions into my journal, and that is when I received in my spirit this love letter from God:

Dear Lisa,

Your times are in My hands, and so are your children. For years I have waited for you to come to Me, to reach for Me instead of the bottle, the drugs, or the men. Only I know and can fulfill the desires of your heart; and when you ask Me for forgiveness, you shall receive it.

I hung on the cross to reconcile all humanity to God, and I would have done it if you were the only person on earth. That is how much I love you.

Your children are in heaven with their Abba Daddy
awaiting the arrival of their earthly mother where there
will be reconciliation. They love you, and so do I.

Afterward, a moment of clarity came. I realized that only Jesus can heal broken people. It is because of His shed blood that the blood on my hands was able to be washed away. When I stood before him, I was as white as the newly fallen snow. But our mind is the battlefield where the war of sin occurs. Things like therapy, counseling, and Twelve Step recovery can plow up the ground of your heart and get you ready for forgiveness. But it is when we repent and confess our sins that God is faithful to forgive us (1 John 1:9).

All of my relapses in recovery, especially the final one, created a desperation that helped me comprehend the concept of renewing my mind through the Word of God. My mind had to be in a renewed state before I could handle the suppressed trauma of my abortions. God never, ever wastes a single hurt.

For so many years after my abortions, I was pro-choice. All I had been doing was distancing myself from the reality of what I did. I had repressed these feelings so deeply that it was almost as though they didn't exist. There are many women and some men who say they have no regrets from their abortion, and I believe they speak prematurely; because I had no regrets either, until I wanted to have a child, and then the reality of my choices just about devoured me.

Until we come to grips with our past and fully surrender we are not free. Bernard Nathanson came face to face with his past when his research discovered that the fetus feels pain at seven weeks of gestation. And that he had inflicted a painful execution on five thousand babies, including one of his own children. However, it wasn't until both Bernie and I yielded that the Lord delivered us from the pain of our past and began to bless us with peace.

Once God releases a blessing, it cannot be revoked; it can lie dormant but will always have the capability to be activated. The time of activation depends on you. Have you ever asked yourself how much you are willing to sacrifice for your relationship with God? God will allow you to get as intimate with Him as you want to be. The closer you get to Him, the more you will look like Him. Resemblance is inevitable because DNA never forgets. But how far would I go? What would I sacrifice? Forgiveness is an unfathomable thing! In it you can find strength, peace, and rest, but this outcome is totally up to you. You can be given a gift, but you have to unwrap it to utilize it. Although I believed in God's grace and forgiveness, I still found it difficult, due to years of abuse, to trust that He had my best interests at heart when it came to me becoming a mom. I complained a lot about not being able to get pregnant. Remember me, the girl who was not only addicted to drugs, but to instant gratification?

In the summer of 1993, while attending one of my regular Twelve Step recovery meetings, I had a monumental awakening. We were studying the Seventh Step: "Humbly asked Him to remove our shortcomings." It explains how the only thing that can transform failure and misery is humility. That self-centered fear is what promotes the attitude that prohibits us from moving closer to God, and really trusting him. About halfway through the meeting it hit me like a lightning bolt: I had more in my life at that very moment than I ever thought I could have or even wanted. I had a loving God in my life who provided serenity and sobriety. My husband loved and respected

> Once God releases a blessing, it cannot be revoked.

me. Contentment and gratitude flooded my soul, filling up the empty space with love and appreciation.

But nothing short of continuous action on this way of thinking will keep you free. So even though I had accepted humility as a necessary aid to survival, still month after month if I was a day late I thought, *Maybe I am pregnant,* only to crash into unyielding disappointment. My solution was to quit hoping. Women who have been waiting to conceive know exactly what I mean. So when I was feeling tired and nauseous, I blamed it on the flu—until it persisted. A friend who had two children urged me to take a pregnancy test, but I couldn't bring myself to do it. I just didn't want to endure the disappointment again. But I had come to a decision: either God was everything or He was nothing, and He would be with me no matter what. So I did it.

Five minutes is an eternity when you are waiting. There I sat, staring in astonishment at a positive result. I just couldn't believe it. Was I dreaming? Wanting to make sure I was reading the test correctly, I called the toll-free help number on the test kit. Through tears and sobs I asked the representative, "Is there any way that if the test strip reads positive I am not pregnant?"

The woman on the other end of the line was compassionate but dead wrong about my emotion: "Oh, ma'am, I am sorry, but if the test strip reads positive, then you are absolutely pregnant."

In just moments, I again experienced God's undeserved and overwhelming grace and mercy. But this was different; it was epic! Years of torment and remorse, sadness and grief were insignificant compared to God's redemption. Tom and I were absolutely, positively overcome with gratitude!

In March 1994 my precious little angel Lily Ann entered this world and immediately stole my heart. Becoming a mother is an immeasurable endowment that transcends time. There is nothing that can compare to the joy and astonishment of hold-ing your baby in your arms for the very first time. She wasn't a mistake, an inconvenience, an accident, or a problem. She was a miracle!

The true meaning of unconditional love began to explain itself. It was the total dependence that she had on me and the ability to give of myself in an extraordinary way. Minute by minute, those hours, weeks, and months added up to create a lifetime of beauty.

By God's abundant grace, it wasn't long before, without even really trying, we were expecting again. My joy doubled in December 1996 when Steven Adam made his debut. His super-sweet temperament grabbed hold of my heart and still has not let go. Watching my children grow and develop has been an awesome experience, one that today I wouldn't trade for anything. Still, there are times when I reflect and remember that I gave up the birthright of five other children because I thought they would be an inconvenience. Oh, how I regret that! What I have discovered is that children aren't an interference from important things; they are the important thing! Somehow in this greedy world of having it all, the simplistic beauty of being a mother is lost. I never really knew my capacity to love until I had my children. My children motivate, challenge, and inspire me. They remind me of why I was put on this earth.

In our family, the chain of self-destruction has been bro-ken. My children will face their future accepting life-affirming boundaries and with deep respect for the sanctity of human life. My children will have the ability to derive joy and satisfaction from all that life has to offer without ever seeing their mother drunk, high, or under any mind-altering substance except love.

Motherhood is a calling that can be met by any woman who will give consistent unconditional love. It doesn't mat-ter whether the child is hers biologically or not. You can be a mother to a person of any age. It is a state of mind, a conviction, an attitude. Perhaps you had women in your life who were like a mother to you. I am thankful that God placed a few women in my life who were happy to fill that role. They each had a loving heart and were full of care and compassion in the good times and the bad. They provided guidance and gave me the courage to attempt things I had never done before. They were women who provided a place for me to come in and find shelter from the storms of life.

> Showing motherly love is overriding your wants and needs for the good of another.

Everyone needs an authentic connection with another person. But to have true authenticity, there must be vulnerability. Motherhood is the ultimate vulnerability. It has been said that out of your vulnerabilities comes your strength. And being a mother takes a lot of strength—the Incredible Hulk kind of strength! Showing motherly love is overriding your wants and needs for the good of another. It's being able to ignite a fire deep within someone else and keep it burning by adding reassuring fuel to that fire. A mother is a woman who makes you feel good about yourself.

God has given women authority through motherhood—not only as it relates to giving guidance and direction or providing care, but also because being a mom allows us to flourish into magnificent, incredible people that we couldn't have become without experiencing the role of motherhood. It is part of our make-up, our spiritual DNA.

A mother's greatest masterpiece is her children.

22

KATHY

Breaking the Cycle

"The beginning of love is
to let those we love be perfectly themselves
and not to twist them to fit our own image."

~Thomas Merton

Lisa first told me about Twelve Step programs while we were
neighbors in Virginia. In fact, at her suggestion I did attend one
recovery meeting for families and friends of alcoholics. I didn't
have any idea what the meetings were actually for, and everyone
was so friendly that when it came my time to share I dumped
my entire life story on those poor people. And then I never went
back. For some strange reason, I didn't seem to get any benefit
out of the program . . . from my one meeting!

Now in Texas, when Mandy suggested I try attending
Twelve Step meetings with her, this time it was a different
story. This time I kept my mouth shut and my ears open. The
group met on the second story of a run-down old building, and
every Tuesday night we'd walk up a rickety set of steps with fin-
gers crossed, hoping they wouldn't collapse. A recovery meeting
for alcoholics and drug addicts met in the front room at the

same time as our meeting, and they would greet us boisterously as we made our way to the back room where people struggling with codependency met. I had no clue how to handle all that enthusiasm from that jolly group of former alcoholics and drug addicts. I'd hurry to the back, smiling and nodding, trying to avoid eye contact.

Never had I experienced any group like this before. These people represented every age group, race, religion, and economic class. Men and women were brutally honest about their lives, and many of their experiences were extreme. Many were dealing with heartbreaking circumstances. They talked about the Twelve Steps, they talked about solutions to grave situations, and they talked about their own attitudes. They spoke openly without shame, and they laughed a lot. They laughed at themselves, laughed about all the ridiculous things they had done to try to control others, and they even laughed about their absurd circumstances. And as for those cliché slogans Lisa kept telling me, I learned that they put those slogans to work in the harsh reality of their daily lives. The one thing they didn't talk about was things other people had done or were doing to them. Often I would think, *How are these folks not curled up somewhere in a mental hospital or raging and complaining about the problems they are dealing with?*

I saw a lot of hope there and wanted the joy and serenity they had, so I asked Mandy to sponsor me through studying and applying the Steps. We started meeting regularly. Several times a week I'd dial her up and spill out the "latest" frustration or injustice in my life.

"You'll never believe what those boys did today."

"I just can't believe we didn't get a raise! It's so unfair."

"Mandy, just how can I get my husband to change?"

"Can you believe what 'they' said this time?" Any "they" would do.

She would patiently listen to me complain and then redirect me to the principles in the Steps. Principles like honesty and acceptance, willingness and humility, faith and courage, and service to others. Then she'd help me look at my own part. "Just keep your side of the street clean, Kathy, and don't worry about theirs," she'd say. Then she'd sign off with her typical farewell: "Cheer up. It'll probably get worse. I love ya!"

Money was still tight, and Dave was slammed with work and travel. Soon after our move I asked him if it would help if I took over the finances. Relieved, he handed over the bills. Now if you remember, the last time I looked through our bills I wound up having a nervous breakdown! So for the first week dealing with our finances my anxiety ran a little high. I organized a schedule and estimated how much money we had for different categories. Every morning I jolted awake with a new fear about the money. *Did I budget for taxes? When are they due? What about school fees? What if a major appliance breaks? Did I remember to pay the water bill?* After a week of waking up with a new fear every day, I put some of what I was learning into practice and told myself to knock it off. God was going to take care of us.

So I kept slugging away at trying to apply these simple truths to my life. They were simple, but they weren't easy. One of the great things about intentionally going through and practicing the principles of the Steps is the opportunity to write out a fearless and searching moral inventory. Take a long look at my life and discover resentments, fears, and how I've harmed others. This was new for me. I mean, I did try to look at my part, but I sure liked taking your inventory at the same time! This process required me to put aside what others had done and bring the focus squarely on myself.

I discovered that I had a big problem applying the "live and let live" principle. In other words, I thought the people in my life were so connected to me that everything they did or thought affected me or reflected on me. I didn't know how to live my own life, and I sure didn't know how to let them live theirs.

This really hit home when it came to my extended family. We believed so differently on things that deeply mattered to me. I still felt a void that I wanted filled with validation. By getting busy with my own life, it was a huge relief to discover that life really could be OK without having everyone agree with my way of seeing things. I also began to realize how demanding I had been, wanting approval from others. When I didn't get that affirmation, I would complain about it to someone else. I would categorize this as "working things out verbally," while the plain truth was I was gossiping. And gossip doesn't solve anything. The more I judged others, the harder I was on myself. I began to work through some of these glaring defects, turning them over to God because I certainly couldn't fix them myself. Perfectionism and trying harder only led to anxiety, isolation, and failure.

> Perfectionism and trying harder only led to anxiety, isolation, and failure.

Then I came to the place in the Steps where it was time for me to make amends to those I had hurt. The prospect of facing people and admitting my wrongs and resolving to live differently was a little nerve-wracking. What would they say? How would they react? Nervously I made phone calls and set up appointments to meet with each individual. Almost without fail, the other person was gracious. Let me tell you, those conversations went way better than the ones where I was trying to force my perspective!

It was a good thing I was getting some emotional and physical relief by making amends because resentments and unfinished business can be exhausting. I had my hands full just managing what was right in front of my own nose. Our house was certainly chaotic with four boys and their antics, and I am what you might call a multitasker. I'm not saying that's a good thing. My husband was constantly trying to keep everyone in line, poor guy—it was like herding cats. Lisa still laughs recalling one visit to our home. Apparently, as she tells it, I was cooking dinner, directing someone with their piano practice, and making biscuits when I dropped everything and ran to the garage with flour on my hands to help one of the boys with their bike chain. She sat there, watching the whole circus and shaking her head. When I came back in I looked at her and asked, "Now, what was I doing?"

Putting these new principles into action really became imperative when our sons headed into their teen years. We could smell trouble brewing. Calls were coming in from their school for missed homework and truancy. "Mrs. Gray, if you could just sit with them every evening and make sure they do all their homework . . ." I remember thinking, *Ma'am, I already passed the eighth grade! Now you want me to hover and hold their hand, checking all their work?*

Believe me, we were already enforcing plenty of rules to help them with boundaries. And every boundary seemed like a new challenge for them to test! By the time they were in high school they had begun making a habit of climbing out an upstairs window and onto the roof to smoke in the middle of the night—smoking, of course, was absolutely forbidden. Other times, while we were sound asleep, they would shimmy down the side of the house, sneak out to party, and shimmy back up before we knew they'd been gone. Neighbors would reluctantly tell us they had caught them in the act. On the upside, we were impressed with their climbing skills!

On the downside, I was losing all sense of control. I was still putting a good chunk of my self-worth in how successful my kids were. Certainly it's natural to hope for our kids to succeed. Parents rightly take on the responsibility of helping our children grow into productive, adjusted adults. The problem is that then we feel responsible when they don't meet our expectations. Well, my feeling of responsibility was on steroids—after all, I was in a program for people who are codependent.

On the outside people saw me as peaceful and easygoing, but inside I was full of worry and self-blame. Lisa, on the other hand, wore all her feelings on her sleeve. I had just as much angst as she did but hid it inside. We both needed to deal with the root causes. For me, worry and resentment showed up disguised as physical maladies. I had migraines, contracted shingles, and had so much tension in my shoulders I couldn't turn my neck. It is true that alcohol and drugs can kill you, but so can unresolved anger, resentment, and anxiety!

Raising teens is when I really buckled down on detaching—separating my feelings from the circumstances, dealing with my fear before making decisions so I could at least have a shot at responding rather than reacting, and then turning the results over to God. Before long, it became obvious we were dealing with more than teenage boy shenanigans. One of our sons was seriously struggling with alcoholism and cocaine addiction.

Over the years Lisa and I had continued to call regularly and traveled to see each other. I would fly out to lead the music at a women's retreat she organized. She would fly out here to speak at Twelve Step gatherings. We always supported each other, but this was when I really leaned on her experience, strength, and hope. Many times I was tempted to let myself crumble into full anxiety, anger, or panic. *This just wasn't what I signed up for!* But I had fallen apart twice before, and I did not want to go through that again. So I would pray, turn it over to God, borrow strength from others, and get busy doing the next right thing.

In the midst of daily dealing with an alcoholic teen, I was consciously concentrating on letting go of my expectations for my extended family. There was a deep root of distortion when it came to my expectations, and I talked about it frequently with my sponsor. One day Mandy, probably tired of hearing me obsess, came up with an idea.

I couldn't fathom not trying to fix the situation.

"I want you to take out a piece of paper and write down what your life would look like if you never interacted with your extended family again." Long pause.

"I don't get the assignment. Seriously, could you repeat the question?"

What would my life be like without my extended family? I didn't even know where to start! I couldn't imagine my life without them. I couldn't fathom not trying to fix the situation. By this time my siblings didn't want anything to do with me, and things just weren't getting better. Mandy explained that she wasn't suggesting I break ties with my family, she was just trying to help me shake loose of my obsession and see myself and them in a different light.

I'd had enough experience by now to know the benefit of taking direction, even when I thought she was nuts. So I pulled out a piece of paper and with pen in hand sat down and stared at it. Nothing was coming. Nada. And then I had one of those *aha* moments.

In Twelve Step groups we are all on a level playing field; no one is superior or inferior, and no one is in charge. We cooperate, taking turns leading. We all give each other the right to live our own lives and respect each other's right to disagree. Right then it hit me. *It didn't matter what each of us in our family thought— everyone has the dignity and the right to their own opinion. We could each believe however we thought was best.* What I realized was, if I could practice this with my Twelve Step comrades, I could apply it to my extended family. Actually, I could practice it with everyone! Real joy and relief flooded me as I laid the struggle to rest. I was free, and so were they. An enormous load lifted off of me that day. And although we have had our ups and downs over the years since, today I enjoy a close and mutually respectful restored relationship with my parents.

Many times my brother's last words resonate in my mind: "I'm in a rut, and I'll never get out. You've done it right." Nobody does it 100 percent right, but what we did get right together is that slogan I had come to cherish: "Live and let live." I was practicing with him all those years ago what I was finally learning to practice with everyone else. He was free to be exactly who he was with me, and I was free to be myself too. We didn't just "get along" or "see things the same way," giving an illusion of being close. I realized that we were close! We had a healthy and mutually respectful relationship with each other. I just hadn't realized it. Seeing that I had compared a real relationship with a perfectionistic fantasy brought great relief to the anxiety I had carried all these years, feeling like I had failed him.

We never know what effect our willingness to change might have. I believe something intangible but real shifted when I truly let go. Not long after that, one of my sisters, the one closest to me in age, pulled me aside at a family gathering and told me she was starting to see things differently. She wanted to have a relationship with me again and asked for my forgiveness. I was shocked. I was also elated! After having laid down my expectations, this was something I thought would never happen. But I sure am glad it did. And the timing couldn't have been better because she became a source of comfort as we headed into the darkest days with our drug-addicted son.

He had started his senior year of high school, but his drug use was so out of control that we could no longer let him live with us. He knew that we would help him as soon as he truly wanted help—but he also knew that he would have to absolutely convince us he was ready and willing. One night after the boys had gone upstairs to bed I was folding laundry in the living room. I folded the clothes, like I'd done for years, out of habit putting them in four separate piles. One for each boy. After a few minutes I looked down at the piles on the coffee table and realized only three spots were being filled. *One of my boys is missing.* Grief welled up in me, and I stumbled outside and sat by the backyard pool. I wept and wept. *Oh, God! Go after my boy. Go get him! He's going to die if You don't do something! You have got to reach him! No one else can.*

A month later the phone rang, and our son wanted to meet us at a nearby Wendy's. Dave took his lunch break, and the three of us sat at a window table. Sitting in front of us our son was haggard and had wasted to eighty-five pounds.

"Mom and Dad," he said, "I need help. I'm ready to get help."

We had done all the paperwork in advance for a rehab facility a few hours away, and had it just ready and waiting for him to finally come to the end of himself—to hit rock bottom. By noon the next day we walked him across the dirt "lawn" and through the front door of a converted house in an older neighborhood. What the facility lacked in glamour it made up for in solid recovery. He sobered up, was immersed in the principles of surrender leading to freedom, and completed an entire year of high school in three months. Six months later we moved him back to Dallas, the city he still calls home. Today he is a thriving entrepreneur and living a full life by the principles he learned during that time. Thinking back, that shabby home looks like Buckingham Palace to me, because it's the place our boy got his life back.

Living out the principles through tough experiences like this, now I was starting to sound like those incredible people

I met when I first started attending meetings. I was the one laughing now, not taking myself too seriously, and learning to actually trust God in every aspect of my life. The cycle of perfectionism and comparison became a thing of the past—most of the time!

Even so, I was constantly getting new scenarios to practice my change of perspective. Our other sons were now attending a prestigious religious private school, and most of the families were in a much higher economic bracket than we were. These people were energetic, kind, and for the most part their kids were well adjusted and doing great. I didn't know anyone there who had lived through our kind of problems. Boy, was I grateful for my friends in my recovery meetings.

We are "only as sick as our secrets."

I had learned that we are "only as sick as our secrets," and it was understood in our family that we didn't have to hide or lie to appear better than we were. One thing I didn't count on was that at any moment some of our painful experiences could be right out there for everyone to see. One evening I was sitting in the audience waiting for a school chorale concert to begin. Before the choir came on stage, their director read several anonymous essays the students had written about "Amazing Grace," one of the songs they'd be performing. She read inspiring and heartfelt essays where students expressed pride for their fathers in the military or how their faith strengthened them to succeed. And then she read a selection that I knew at once was written by one of our younger sons. It began like this,

"The amazing grace in my life is a strange one. I am the younger brother of an alcoholic. For years he took out his anger on me, putting me down and hurting me in any way he could . . ." The essay went on to share how this brother had gotten into rehab and how during a family meeting he had asked the younger brother for forgiveness. It ended with, "Now we are best friends, and that is the amazing grace in my life."

Tears spilled out as soon as I heard "younger brother of an alcoholic" and didn't stop until the end of the concert. My chest ached with the pain of the past, his pain. I also felt conspicuous, so different from everyone else. We stood out like a sore thumb. I called a friend on my way home, and she reassured me, "I'm telling you, someone in that audience needed to hear that. I'm proud of him for writing so honestly from his heart! That took a lot of courage."

Another truth began taking root in my life: you can't keep it unless you give it away. Women with similar struggles began asking to meet with me. I tell them the same truths I was told, and I still grin as I hear them tell the same tales of woe that I used to share with my sponsor. Because of the truths I've learned sitting in those rooms of recovery and putting them to the test in my own life, I have some real solutions to offer, not just advice or solving their problems for them. I don't have to fix anything for them. That's God's job, not mine!

Today, my deep passion for helping other hurting women reminds me so much of my brother. Steve felt great passion about physically helping those in need. He struggled with what he felt was an intellectual spirituality in the Christian community that didn't meet what he considered "real needs." In our conversations it was clear he wanted to act from his heart, not his head, and he was looking for a balance between the two. Because between our heart and head is where intuition lies, and he was deeply intuitive. He wanted to be in the trenches handing out food, aiding the elderly, helping veterans and the homeless. Injustice angered him, and we used to talk about how he struggled to reconcile his relationship with God and all the pain he encountered, even pain within himself.

Letting go of resentments and obsessive worry frees up a lot of time and energy. New opportunities were opening up that I never dreamed I'd be involved in. One day in 2011, Lisa called me to say she was going to host a weekly Internet radio show, spreading experience, strength, and hope by interviewing guests who had overcome hardships in their lives. I told her I thought that was a great idea! That is until she asked me to be one of her first guests.

"Lisa, you don't want me! I mean, I can't be on the radio! Who would want to hear what I have to say?"

The truth was I was afraid. Not all the kinks had been worked out with fear of failure! But like usual, Lisa persuaded me to come around to her way of thinking and convinced me to come on as a guest. And we had a blast. Then she batted away my protests when she asked me to come on as a long distance cohost once a month. It wasn't long before I found myself cohosting full time, and we were engaging in rich and inspiring conversations with outstanding guests. It still makes me laugh when I think about Lisa's way of talking me into taking risks. I sure am glad she does.

One week when I was unable to cohost due to a prior commitment, she interviewed a guest who introduced her to the life of Dr. Bernard Nathanson. As soon as the show ended my phone rang. Lisa was shaken. Her words tumbled out as she told me the unbelievable impact this man had on our culture, and on her. I stood still, holding the phone, dumbfounded. That a physician had been behind the decriminalization of abortion absolutely blew my mind. I just couldn't believe a man who had taken an oath to "do no harm" could have been so obsessed with legalizing abortion, only to completely change his mind ten years later! I began researching everything I could find out about this man who did so much to endanger the unborn and then turned around and devoted his life to protecting them.

Over the next few months following Lisa's radio interview, I found myself in a perfect storm of events that included hosting the leaders of a national organization dedicated to praying the end of legalized abortion into reality. In April 2012 I stood in front of the US District Courthouse in Dallas, where *Roe v. Wade* had been filed thirty-nine years earlier. Surrounded by thousands of people from all walks of life, we prayed for an end to the extinction of our most vulnerable citizens, the unborn. They talked about adoption, care for pregnant women, resources to help mothers who chose to keep their babies. They talked about resources for women and men who had chosen abortion, praying as well for the doctors and workers in abortion clinics.

Women spoke of their own experiences. My heart ached as women wept in agony over the loss of their own children through abortion. It was an agony I was all too familiar with, having mentored many women struggling through that same anguish. The same anguish that Lisa had experienced. I called Lisa the next day, and we discussed the impact Bernard Nathanson had had, not only in America but in her life personally. We talked about how no one seemed to know who he was and the shady way he had contributed to abortion. I hung up the phone and knew that my life and Lisa's life would once again intersect for a higher purpose.

23

BERNIE

It's All about Love

> "Forgiveness unleashes joy.
> It brings peace. It washes the slate clean.
> It sets all the highest values of love in motion. In a sense,
> forgiveness is Christianity at its highest level."
>
> ~George MacDonald

"I saw a man kneeling on the marble floor in front of the altar. He was older. And he was absolutely still. As I looked at him, I could sense the presence of God. That man was Bernie Nathanson."

Sitting in a church office with a beautiful view on a crisp autumn morning in 2014, Lisa and Kathy hung on every word as Deacon Keith Fournier described his first encounter with Bernie Nathanson nearly twenty years earlier. The energetic, smiling, articulate deacon poured out story after story, giving a rare personal account of Bernie's life after his conversion. His love for his friend was palpable, and his eyes shone while he recalled the details and essence of this remarkable man. They sat spellbound, furiously taking notes, grateful for the deacon who had generously carved time out of his busy schedule to meet with them. He was given the privilege of friendship with Bernie from the beautiful turning point to faith through the remainder of his life.

Bernie knew that he'd made a mess of his life and had willingly surrendered control to Christ. He realized he was now in God's hands. He had reached the end of his personal desperation. He had come to not just believe, but to know that he was forgiven—a conviction that both Kathy and Lisa had finally experienced as well. Bernie had at last been alive—reborn. Relief from inner torment gave him his first opportunity to truly rest after struggling for all his life, really. Finally, he could bask in the warmth of belonging after decades of feeling cold and alone. He had truly become a part of a vibrant community of faith, complete with brothers and sisters and even fathers. So with his newfound freedom, what exactly did Dr. Bernard Nathanson do with the rest of his life?

> Relief from inner torment gave him his first opportunity to truly rest.

Before we finish his story, how about you? What would you do? What would your life be like if you knew you were forgiven? For everything? Really knew it—felt it and lived in the glow of that reality. Often, the most difficult part of forgiveness is actually forgiving oneself. We enslave ourselves to the *if onlys* and *how could I haves.* Desperate to earn a clean conscience, we spin our wheels striving to make up for how we've harmed others, throw our hands up in exhaustion, only to rally and try again. Have you ever carried around a heavy weight of guilt over past actions or past failures?

After Lisa and Tom were married, she anxiously waited, month by month, for years to become pregnant. She felt like a failure. If only her past had been different. If only she hadn't smoked the first joint, snorted the first line, or turned the first trick. Maybe if she had met Tom before all this she would have never made the decision to abort her babies, and they would be alive and full of hope. She carried a deep sense of regret and guilt that kept her from becoming all that she was created to be.

Kathy would agonize over how she dragged her husband and boys, friends and extended family through the trauma of her breakdowns. As her head would hit the pillow, regret would seize her chest and aching heart, and she would wish she could go back and change things. The *if onlys* plagued her too: If only she hadn't been so stubborn, pushing so hard to fix broken family relationships. If only she hadn't been consumed with fear that she would fail as a mother and ruin her sons' lives. If only she hadn't compared herself with everyone around her, failing to measure up or feeling smugly superior in her own mind. If only she had believed God really would take care of everything. If only she hadn't pushed herself over the edge and taken herself out of commission for the people she loved the most.

Regret over lost opportunities, lost relationships, and even lost lives can eat away at our energy for today and steal our vision for the future. Refusing to receive forgiveness sets us up as judge and jury over ourselves and is in reality one of the highest forms of arrogance. Unforgiveness derails us from our destiny—even if it is toward ourselves. But it doesn't feel that way. It disguises itself as humility and determination to do what is right. By refusing to agree with God and forgive ourselves we say, "I know better than God. I decide when I've made up for my past." As C. S. Lewis wisely penned, "I think that if God forgives us we must forgive ourselves. Otherwise, it is almost like setting up ourselves as a higher tribunal than Him."[1] The true nature of humility is aligning ourselves with our Creator and believing what He tells us is true.

Bernie Nathanson came to believe that because Jesus, the Son of God, had died and paid for his sins, he was forgiven. His debt was paid. And here's the twist: because his debt was paid he felt eternally indebted to the One who bought his freedom. He never took it for granted. Bernie's conscience was finally relieved, but his heart never forgot the seriousness of his crimes. He accepted that he was forgiven and let it take root in his soul. Bernie was like the Apostle Paul who had murdered numerous followers of Jesus. Paul later became a believer himself, but he never forgot what he had done. Jesus Himself said whoever is forgiven much, loves much (Luke 7:47).

Captured on video giving one of his many addresses, Dr. Nathanson shared slowly and deliberately, "I stand before you as a mass murderer. I am directly responsible for the deaths of 75,000 innocent children . . . And I want to tell you that is a daunting prospect, a heavy moral baggage to bring into the next world."[2] His expression is one of somber, agonized remorse.

The doctor's heart was both softened and emboldened through forgiveness. Renewed by fresh energy he worked harder than ever to save as many lives as possible. Never believing that age was limiting, Bernie earned a degree in bioethics from Vanderbilt University in 1996 at the age of seventy. He burned with a passion for the law, wanting to speak out for those who couldn't speak for themselves, the unborn. He even considered attending law school. He became a staunch advocate of life at its earliest stages, and served as an expert witness in court cases involving abortion. He believed medical science was the greatest ally to save the unborn and possessed a prophetic capacity to articulate that. Bernie traveled the globe giving dozens of lectures and encouraging those in the fight to save lives still in the womb, the most vulnerable citizens in the world.

In addition, this former Jewish atheist, now a grateful Roman Catholic, fervently encouraged collaborative work between Catholics and Protestants. Personally encouraged by Bernie in this shared passion, Deacon Fournier expressed it beautifully to Lisa and Kathy when they interviewed him, pointing out that the silver lining within the cloud of death is solidarity between Catholics and Protestants in the trenches.

Having at last found his home, you might even say having finally come home, Bernie immersed himself in his Christian community, his new family. He was a faithful, active member of his local parish and joined his newfound brothers on spiritual retreats. Integrity now became non-negotiable for this former liar who had lived a life of contradictions and intentional dishonesty. His life became

> Because his debt was paid he felt eternally indebted to the One who bought his freedom.

integrated, without hypocrisy. The same Bernie Nathanson showed up, whether conferring with fellow physicians, talking with his priest, answering a question from a participant in a conference, or greeting his local grocer. His mannerisms were blunt and sometimes brusque, but those close to Bernie describe him as a warm and interested man. He cared about others, always asking them what they were thinking. His friendships were genuine and deep as he grew in his life of faith. Bernie's extreme intelligence was, at the end of his life, balanced by genuine humility, a rare combination, and those who encountered him were forever changed. Because of his growing closeness to his Creator, born out of surrender, he became a man without guile who had absolutely no tolerance for pretense. He'd had enough lies for one lifetime! Bernard Nathanson was now all about love.

After years of showcasing the devastation of deception, Bernie became a living example of what happens to a person in the presence of the redemption and generosity of a loving Father. Twisted and scarred by a love-starved home, spending much of his life cut off from affection, he found the kind of love he had always longed for. His spiritual transformation opened the door for him to step out on the stage and take the lead role in a genuine love story. The same year he was baptized, he married a loving, beautiful, and talented woman with whom he shared the remainder of his life. Theirs was a marriage of devotion, shared faith, loyalty, laughter, and tender affection. True to their vows, "in sickness and in health," she nursed him with love, humor, and song through a long battle with cancer.

A man restored and loved, Bernie made his final journey home to his Father in heaven on February 21, 2011, memorialized and celebrated by his many brothers and sisters in the faith. Along with Lisa's children who are "in heaven with their Abba Daddy awaiting the arrival of their earthly mother," we imagine a joyful Bernie surrounded by and reconciled now to millions of other children, finally getting to love each precious one.

24

The Rest of the Story

Every individual who has graced this earth from the beginning of time was born for one purpose: love. We were created by love. We were created for love. Love is written in our DNA—it is the very foundation of our identity.

God is love. Not only is He love, He is the light of the world. Whoever follows Him will no longer walk in darkness but will have the light of life.[1] We can't make ourselves our own light. The only way we can be filled with light is through a relationship with Jesus. He weaves Himself through us, allowing the light of truth to shine in our hearts.

But deception blocks the light of truth, leaving us lost in our own darkness—and we don't even know we are in the dark! When we were promised that "the right to choose" was a solution that ensured freedom for women and future generations, we got darkness. We lost an entire generation; in its place we have a country full of women struggling to find their way.

But the good news is there is hope. No one life is superior or more valuable than another. There are no "throwaway lives." Every life is precious to God and to us. Every person is created with a unique once-in-an-eternity gift mix that only he or she will ever possess. Each of us has a contribution to make, that only we can make. Each of us is a vital piece of the whole. Without you, without me, the puzzle is missing pieces and the picture is incomplete. Perhaps you are struggling through a divorce or working double time as a single parent. You are not forgotten. Whether you are homeless, an inmate, or newly released from incarceration, you are valuable. If you're an addict, alcoholic, or struggling with mental illness, your life matters. If you are a veteran, elderly, or physically disabled, you are significant. And to the most vulnerable of all humanity, the unborn, you are indispensable. In America every human being has the right to life, liberty, and pursuit of happiness.

> Every person is created with a unique once-in-an-eternity gift mix that only he or she will ever possess.

Americans are passionate about life. We are the first and perhaps the only nation that holds as self-evident truths that all men and women are created equal and are endowed by their Creator with unalienable rights. It is at the heart of who we are. We are a nation that cheers for the underdog. We love a come-from-behind story. The popular movie *Forrest Gump* won six Academy Awards—a story championing a man with learning disabilities raised by a single mother, who rose above his challenges and, through determination and courage, showed that love conquers all. We support and legislate for child safety and celebrate family. We cry out against domestic violence and child abuse.

In ancient societies, however, violence and child sacrifice were a way of life. Communities were built on it; kings openly supported and encouraged it. Molech, a widely worshipped deity, was known by different names in many cultures. He was revered as the controller of war and fertility; he was the god of protection and insurance of the next generation. His statue was a towering hollow iron figure of an enormous man with the head of a bull and arms outstretched. Sexual promiscuity was encouraged in the worship of Molech, which resulted in pregnancies and unwelcome infants.[2]

In an effort to secure prosperity, Molech's leaders would host a ceremony. They would begin by building a massive fire in the belly of the statue, heating the metal to a glowing red. The community would gather, bringing their four-to-six-week-old infants. Thunderous drums and shrill flutes would fill the air. Leaders would place the infants in the fiery hot arms of the statue. The screams of the child, who was literally being burnt alive, would be drowned out by the deliberate beating of the drums, deafening the mothers to the cries of their children. Just as horrifying was the everyday practice of foundational sacrifices. When a family constructed a home, their newborn would be slaughtered and built into the foundation of the structure to insure good luck for future family members.[3]

Is it possible we are doing exactly the same thing? Is history repeating itself? But surely we're much more sophisticated than these ancient societies: we don't build ridiculous statues and burn our babies alive! However, we cherish our sexual freedom, so our unwanted babies are slaughtered in secret, cloaked in the guise of a medical procedure. Could it be that we are so dedicated to a standard of living that we feel it necessary to eliminate anything that may jeopardize it? Anything including an unwanted pregnancy, even if it that means sacrificing our own baby? Is our individual pursuit of happiness blocking the light of truth? Perhaps we convince ourselves our motives are more considerate and humane. Wanting a secure foundation for our future, have we bought into the lie that we must end an untimely pregnancy so we can prepare to be a parent at a more advantageous time? Is this any different than the ancient practice of parents burying their baby in the structure of their home to bring them good luck in the future?

Yet, we as a nation adamantly support a woman's right to refuse the first breath to her unborn child. Can you see the disconnect here? Have we broken from our true nature?

When a woman has an abortion, the aftermath is tragic. Dr. Nathanson saw the tragedy but attributed it to the quality of the abortion. He did not recognize the emotional, spiritual, and physical havoc it wreaks on a woman. But the repercussions of an abortion may germinate for years before being recognized. As with Lisa, the fallout often resurfaces as other maladies— addiction, depression, self-harm, poor choices, anger, codependency, suicide, chronic fatigue, and cycles of self-defeating behavior. Abortion is never included by the media in coverage of the real war on women.

Isn't part of the real war on women how we perceive their value? Are we are being conditioned by a cultural mentality, a drum beaten loudly by the media, that women are valued by their external beauty, sexuality, and career success? The truth is every woman is born with inherent value and God-given authority. If she embraces her intrinsic worth she will not feel compelled to define herself through outward accomplishments.

In America we praise celebrity figures for being seductive and overtly sexual. This power is a counterfeit for genuine authority. Take for example the beautiful current pop star Nicki Minaj. This extremely successful and vivacious singer became pregnant in her teens, and she chose abortion. She now admits this has haunted her ever since. No matter how much external success she gains through her talents or fame or sexuality, in her opinion her value is incomplete because of her loss of motherhood. "If I'm done with my fifth album and I don't have a child by then, no matter how much money I have, I would be disappointed as a woman, because I feel like I was put here to be a mother."[4] Regret is a powerful emotion that many women wrestle with for years after their abortion.

Because of the challenges of parenting or the pain of giving up a child for adoption, abortion is often seen as the path of least resistance. When we, as a society, become accustomed to this path we forfeit our sense of duty and honor. Women in this country have been conditioned to believe that choosing to end the life of an unborn child is a courageous decision. But a woman's innate protective instinct is undermined through abortion, and they are lured by "the ease" of abortion into cowardice not courage. This characteristic is far from a woman's true identity. The same kind of cowardice presented itself to Kathy when it tempted her to abandon her children and attempt suicide. Neither women nor men were intended to bear the weight of the power of life and death. That belongs solely to God.

> A woman's innate protective instinct is undermined through abortion.

The argument for abortion that succeeded in granting it legal status was built on the assumption that it wasn't a life; it was a mass of cells, a blob of tissue—just as Bernie believed and Lisa was told. Yet the facts are undeniable. At conception, a baby's DNA is set and most features are determined, including eye color and blood type.[5] Even pro-choice proponents today have accepted this scientific evidence.[6]

So they have shifted the argument. Their argument is actually no longer whether life begins at conception; they have now turned to the nature of "personhood." This speaks of the degree of value placed on one life over another, asserting that the mother's life is more valuable than the child's. It is a diversion tactic, much like the drumbeat distractions during the sacrifices to Molech. Since when do any mother and father choose their own life over saving their child? Somehow we are numb to this gruesome reality simply because of its geographic location in the womb—six inches out of sight. This same "disposable life" philosophy duped Lisa, Bernie, and Kathy, robbing them, for a time, of their self-worth, sanity, and purpose.

Thankfully, millions of Americans devote their time, energy, and resources to better the lives of some who society might consider throwaways. However, self- sacrificing, intelligent, loving people have been blinded to the plight of the unborn. What if laws existed that granted family members the right to choose the untimely death of an elderly relative or disabled child? What if the homeless, transitioning inmates or returning veterans were classified as a burden to society and were subjected to the possibility of euthanasia? We would shriek in horror. But proponents of choice do not recognize this same horror as it relates to abortion. Why are unborn citizens in a class by themselves? What makes this vulnerable people group not worth protecting? It is time for an awakening; it is time for all well-meaning people with integrity to get honest with themselves. Ignoring the value of all people, *including* the life that exists in the womb, is, as Dr. Nathanson said, "the crassest kind of moral evasiveness." Are we courageous enough, like Bernard Nathanson, to change our minds?

Through repentance in Christ, Lisa Kratz Thomas saw the light and overcame the guilt, shame, and remorse of abortion. By devoting herself to dispelling the idea of throwaway lives, Lisa has been able to motivate, inspire, and help post-abortive women, drug addicts, alcoholics, and offenders not only believe that second chances are possible, but attainable. She went from the crack house to the state house, serving on a Senate Sub-Committee that studied prisoner reentry in the state of

Virginia. She founded a non-profit organization called New Vision that provided hope and resources to disenfranchised women who were reentering society from incarceration. This project threw her into reentry advocacy where she continues to this day, visiting close to twenty different prisons annually, sharing hope with both men and women. Not only has she mentored countless women; she is also an advisor and confidant to elected officials, their wives, and clergy. Lisa is real. Due to her restored life and confidence in Christ, she is authentic no matter who she is encouraging.

Emerging from the fog of comparison and perfectionism, Kathy Gray came to value life, all life, even her own. Once deeply deceived into believing some lives were more valuable than others, she has become passionate about helping others get free of enslaving mindsets. Changing her mind and agreeing with God about her intrinsic value and authority, she transformed from a non-functioning, panic-stricken young mother to confidently raising four sons, including weathering the storms of teenage rebellion and drug and alcohol abuse. She has mentored numerous women both inside and outside the rooms of Twelve Step recovery, helping them get free of despair and the effects of past abuse and watching them flourish in the midst of devastating circumstances. Without shame, she shares her story of failure and transformation at conferences and retreats, or one on one at the local coffee shop. An accomplished musician once paralyzed with self-doubt and feeling unqualified to make a contribution in any area of her life, she now pours into the musical development of multiple students. Pushing through her fears and taking the risk of failure, she uses her musical gift to lead people to the heart of God through praise and worship. Instead of waking up dreading the day, she now wakes up thanking God for another day of life, expecting to see His goodness and provision.

Opening his heart to the light allowed Bernard Nathanson to see truth. Everything he did from that day forward, he did because he was changed by love. He was changed by the love of God and others. After years of being the voice for abortion, he declared abortion as murder and became a prominent pro-life proponent. The author of several books, the director of two short films, and a public speaker, he was able to spread the message of life and transformation. His conversion to Catholicism generated change and fulfillment, bringing him out of isolation and into belonging like he had never experienced before. He was a good friend, able to develop meaningful relationships, and loved by many. Built on a foundation of love and forgiveness, he entered a marriage that was full of affection. Through his tireless efforts, he spent the remainder of his life trying to reign in the culture of death that he had unleashed on America. Once full of fear and self-doubt, longing for acceptance, he died a man enveloped by love.

> Repentance is the key that unlocks the door and allows the light to stream in.

Anyone could have looked at Lisa, or Kathy, or Bernie and concluded they were done for—throwaways, in different ways. Yet, who would have thought that a former crackhead prostitute would partner with a broken, mentally unstable suburban housewife, and then come to admire and love a man who was responsible for over 75,000 deaths. Only God! He imprinted it on their DNA. Who would have thought that Lisa and Kathy, formerly as different as night and day, brought together through overcoming pain, dysfunction, and failure would be given the platform to host an international radio show, speaking to the world to bring hope to those who suffer? Through repentance, we can all be restored to our original destiny, clearing our vision and enabling us to regard all people as redeemable and precious. Who would have thought three formerly suicidal individuals would have found hope and strength in God and become obsessed with helping others?

These three lives are examples of divine restoration. God's original DNA in us is more powerful than any mindset or choice we have made. We all long for God, even before we know him. This longing expresses itself in hurtful ways as we try to fill the space in us that only God can fill.

When God's presence fills that space, He weaves His life-giving light in us. His light is filled with hope, healing, courage, and purpose. It enables us to let go of our destructive ways.

Repentance is the key that unlocks the door and allows the light to stream in. But let's not confuse remorse with repentance. Remorse is a feeling of regret, of being sorry for something we've done. Repentance, on the other hand, is an action or a process—a true heart change. Remorse doesn't take responsibility for our actions and is temporary. Repentance empowers us to live differently and experience the joy of living the dream—our true identity.

Darkness steals our ability to live in freedom. Every past mistake, all of our secrets and shame, every wound, every injustice that weighs us down, all of our confusion, all of our anger, our loneliness, the pain that haunts us—lives inside our darkness.

BUT you were created for the light. You were created in the light. You don't have to struggle and strive to live in that light. You were created to be electrifying, to be a part of something vital, something bigger than yourself. You were born to be an indispensable, integral part of your family and community. You were born to thrive. You were born to be a world changer.

You were born to shine!

For you were once darkness,
but now you are light in the Lord.
Walk as children of light.
~Ephesians 5:8

Epilogue

By Deacon Keith Fournier

At the heart of the Christian claim is the bold assertion that every man, woman, and child is created in the Image of God— and loved by the Father. In the words of the Western Bishop Augustine, "Our hearts are restless until they rest in Him." So deep is God's love for us that, as the Apostle Paul wrote, "While we were yet sinners, Christ died for us" (Romans 5:8 KJV).

The Father gave His Son to save us, to free us from the poor choices we make, to heal us from the consequences that follow, and to make us new. We were saved *from* death, and we were saved *for* a new way of living, which begins now!

At the heart of Christian morality is another revolutionary assertion: our freedom is modeled after God's freedom. He wants us to freely respond to His invitations of Love. Real Love never coerces.

But there is a problem; it is referred to theologically as sin.

We turn away from His loving plan, and, as a result of our wrong choices, our capacity to exercise this freedom correctly—by always choosing what is good and beautiful and true—is fractured. We cannot save ourselves from this predicament. We need a Savior.

The Cross of Jesus Christ is the splint that can heal our fractured freedom. Its wood builds the bridge between heaven and earth, and the Way back to the Father. The blood that was shed by the One who willingly stretched out His arms heals the separation that resulted from our sin.

In His Divinity, He did for us what we could never have done for ourselves. In His Sacred humanity, He shows us the road map to a new Way upon which to walk. His empty tomb is the pledge of re-creation in the Resurrection. Its power to transform us begins in this life and opens up to life eternal.

Our choices not only change the world around us, they change us. In a very real sense, we become what we choose. As we cooperate with grace and begin to choose differently, we become what the same Apostle told the Corinthians—new creations in Christ (2 Corinthians 5:17).

How do we communicate this Good News to those living in their self-constructed tombs? How do we offer the liberating promise that there is no pit too deep that God is not deeper, no person too far gone, no man or woman who is outside of the grasp of this God of Amazing Grace and boundless Love?

One of the most effective ways is by putting legs on the Gospel. By telling the stories of real people who were nearly swallowed up by the darkness and death of sin, but found the Way home to the love of the Father, through the Son and in the Spirit—and walked out of the darkness into the light. Men and women who were derailed for a time, but rescued, spiritually and emotionally dead brought back from the dead.

The best of these kinds of conversion stories are the ones that hold nothing back. They paint with real pain. Compelling stories of people who moved from devastation to destiny. *Light in Our Darkness*, by Lisa Kratz Thomas and Kathy Gray, tells such stories. It is gritty and real. It is also a good read that is hard to put down. But most importantly, it offers the hope that comes from the light of the Gospel.

By juxtaposing the stories of three very different people whose lives were changed by encountering the same Risen Christ—and whose choices not only changed the world around them, but changed them, making them new—the authors help to open the eyes of their reader to the Christian claim. They make clear the essential message needed in this urgent hour. Christianity is not some-Thing, but about Some-One, Jesus Christ. He is alive, and encountering Him is available to everyone.

One of the three stories tells of a man whom I had the privilege of calling my friend, Dr. Bernard Nathanson. I was delighted when I heard that the authors wanted to tell the extraordinary story of this modern-day St. Paul to more people. That fact alone opened me to my first meeting with Lisa and Kathy at their request.

When we met, I was able to tell them all about this great champion of the Culture of Life. Then I listened to their own stories. They held out the same promise of the love of a Risen Savior. I was excited about their book project, and stayed in touch.

Now that I have read the book, I am pleased to recommend it to you. The way in which the authors have woven the three stories together and offered the Gospel as the common life rope, which rescued them from the ocean of despair and placed them on a new path, is a compelling book that could change the destiny of many.

Endnotes

Chapter 2

1. "Martin Luther King Birthday Interview with Terry Beatley," *This is Your Life: Courage to Change,* Here Women Talk, Zeus Radio Network, January 16, 2012.

2. See, e.g., Maureen L. Condic, "When Does Human Life Begin? A Scientific Perspective" (Thornwood, NY: The Westchester Institute for Ethics & the Human Person, Oct. 2008), http://bdfund.org/wordpress/wp-content/uploads/2012/06/wi_whitepaper_life_print.pdf.

3. Bedri Karakas et al., (2015) *Noninvasive Digital Detection of Fetal DNA in Plasma of 4-Week-Pregnant Women following In Vitro Fertilization and Embryo Transfer.* PLoS ONE 10(5): e0126501. http://doi.org/10.1371/journal.pone.0126501.

4. Karen Pazol et al., *Morbidity and Mortality Weekly Report,* Abortion Surveillance—United States, 2009; Surveillance Summaries, November 23, 2012/61(SS08); 1–44, Division of Reproductive Health, National Center for Chronic Disease Prevention and Health Promotion, Centers for Disease Control and Prevention, http://www.cdc.gov/mmwr/preview/mmwrhtml/ss6108a1.htm.

5. Bernard N. Nathanson, *The Hand of God: A Journey from Death to Life by the Abortion Doctor Who Changed His Mind* (Fort Collins, CO: Life Cycle Books, 1996), 90.

6. A.W. Liley, "The Foetus as a Personality," *Australian and New Zealand Journal of Psychiatry* 6 (1972): 99.

Chapter 4

1. Liley, "The Foetus as a Personality," 99.

2. Complete Jewish Bible. Copyright © 1988 by David H. Stern.

3. "Joseph N. Nathanson (1895–1989)," McGill University Library Digital Collection, http://digital.library.mcgill.ca/lincoln/nathanson.htm.

4. Nathanson, *Hand of God*, 20.

Chapter 5

1. Donald L. Hilton and Clark Watts, "Pornography Addiction: A Neuroscience Perspective," *Surgical Neurology International* 2 (2011): 19. http://doi.org/10.4103/2152-7806.76977.

Chapter 8

1. Nathanson, *Hand of God*, 24.
2. Ibid., 63.

Chapter 9

1. Nathanson, *Hand of God*, 89.

2. Jone Johnson Lewis, "Abortion History: A Brief History of the Abortion Controversy in the United States," http://womenshistory.about.com/od/abortionuslegal/a/abortion.htm.

3. Nathanson, *Hand of God*, 92.

4.   Bernard Nathanson, "Confessions of an Ex-Abortionist," Catholic Education Resource Center, http://www.catholiceducation.org/en/controversy/abortion/confessions-of-an-ex-abortionist.html.

5.   Nathanson, *Hand of God*, 121–22.

6.   Bernard N. Nathanson and Richard N. Ostling, *Aborting America* (New York: Pinnacle, 1979), 95.

7.   "Abortion Industry Negligence Nationwide," Susan B. Anthony List, http://www.sba-list.org/negligence.

8.   Catherine E. Ross and Janet Lauritsen, "Public Opinion about Doctors' Pay," *American Journal of Public Health* 75 (1985): 668–670. http://www.ncbi.nlm.nih.gov/pmc/articles/PMC1646197/pdf/amjph00282-0094.pdf.

9.   Nathanson, *Hand of God*, 109.

10. Nathanson and Ostling, *Aborting America*, 168.

11. "The Law: Ambivalence on Abortion," *Time*, May 3, 1971.

12. Jason DeParle, "The Worst City Government in America—Washington, D.C.," *Washington Monthly*, January 1989.

13. Nathanson, *Hand of God*, 127.

14. Ibid., 129.

Chapter 11

1.   DeParle, "The Worst City Government in America."

Chapter 12

1.   https://www.facebook.com/TheShackOfficial/photos/pb.766988633389495.-2207520000.1445114307./861611050593919/?type=3&theater.

Chapter 13

1.   Nathanson, *Hand of God*, 152.

2. Bernard Nathanson quoted in D. James Kennedy, *Abortion: A Reflection on Life* (Ft. Lauderdale, FL: Coral Ridge Ministries, 1989), 5.

3. Nathanson, *Hand of God*, 162.

4. David Kupelian, *The Marketing of Evil: How Radicals, Elitists, and Pseudo-Experts Sell Us Corruption Disguised as Freedom* (Washington, DC: WND Books, 2005), 192.

5. Nathanson, *Hand of God*, 131.

6. Nathanson and Ostling, *Aborting America*, 172.

7. Nathanson, *Hand of God*, 130.

8. Dudley Clendinen, "President Praises Foes of Abortion," *New York Times*, January 23, 1985, http://www.nytimes.com/1985/01/23/us/president-praises-foes-of-abortion.html.

9. Nathanson, *Hand of God*, 163–176.

10. Johnson, Walter, M.D., "Don't Be Lulled: Live Fetuses Used in Tissue Transplants," New Earth, 5/93, p. 14. Further reading: (A) Haskell, Martin, M.D., "Second Trimester D and X, 20 Wks and Beyond," National Abortion Federation presentation, 10/92, 10 pages; (B) Hutchinson, Robert, "Fetal Harvesting Insanity," You! 5/93, pp. 20–23, complete with graphic drawings of how the baby's brain cells are extracted prior to the completion of the abortion. As cited by Judie Brown in "Recycling Babies: The Practice of Fetal Tissue Research," American Bioethics Advisory Commission, 1996, http://original.all.org/abac/eg99y.htm.

11. Nathanson, *Hand of God*, 4.

Chapter 17

1. Nathanson and Ostling, *Aborting America*, 165.

2. Bernard N. Nathanson, *The Abortion Papers: Inside the Abortion Mentality* (New York: Frederick Fell, 1983), 5.

3. Nathanson and Ostling, *Aborting America*, 165.

4.   Kupelian, *Marketing of Evil.*

5.   Thomas W. Strahan, "Studies Suggesting That Induced Abortion May Increase the Feminization of Poverty," *Feminism and Nonviolence Studies* 1, no. 3 (1995), http://www.fnsa.org/v1n3/strahan.html.

6.   Christopher Tietze, "Repeat Abortions—Why More?" *Family Planning Perspectives* 10, no. 5 (1978): 286; Stanley K. Henshaw, "Characteristics of U.S. Women Having Abortions, 1982–1983," *Family Planning Perspectives* 1, no. 1 (1987): 5.

7.   Strahan, "Induced Abortion May Increase the Feminization of Poverty."

8.   Kathleen N. Franco, Marijo B. Tamburrino, and Nancy B. Campbell, "Psychological Profile of Dysphoric Women Post-Abortion," *Journal of the American Medical Women's Association* 44, no. 113 (1989); Gail B. Williams, "Induced Elective Abortion and Perinatal Grief," Ph.D. Dissertation, New York University (1991).

9.   Strahan, "Induced Abortion May Increase the Feminization of Poverty."

10. "Symptoms of Post-Abortion Trauma," Rachel's Vineyard, http://www.rachelsvineyard.org/emotions/symptoms.aspx.

11. Mika Gissler, Elina Hemminki, and Jouko Lonnqvist, "Suicides After Pregnancy in Finland, 1987–94: Register Linkage Study," *British Medical Journal* 313 (1996): 1431–1434; M. Gissler, "Injury Deaths, Suicides and Homicides Associated with Pregnancy, Finland 1987–2000," *European Journal of Public Health* 15, no. 5 (2005): 459–463; David C. Reardon, *Aborted Women, Silent No More* (Springfield, IL: Acorn Books, 2002).

12. B. Garfinkel, et al., "Stress, Depression and Suicide: A Study of Adolescents in Minnesota," *Responding to High Risk Youth* (University of Minnesota: Minnesota Extension Service, 1986); Gissler, Hemminki, and Lonnqvist, "Suicides After Pregnancy in Finland," 1431–1434; N. Campbell et al.,

"Abortion in Adolescence," *Adolescence* 23 (1988): 813–823. For more information see the "Teen Abortion Risks" Fact Sheet at http://www.theunchoice.com/pdf/OnePageFactSheets/Teens Sheet1.pdf.

13. V. M. Rue et al., "Induced Abortion and Traumatic Stress: A Preliminary Comparison of American and Russian Women," *Medical Science Monitor* 10, no. 10 (2004): SR5–16.

14. "The Emotional Effects of Induced Abortion," Planned Parenthood, http://www.plannedparenthood.org/files/8413/9611/5708/Abortion_Emotional_Effects.pdf.

15. D. M. Fergusson, L. J. Horwood, and E. M. Ridder, "Abortion in Young Women and Subsequent Mental Health," *Journal of Child Psychology and Psychiatry* 47, no. 1 (2006): 16–24.

16. Theresa Burke with David Reardon, *Forbidden Grief: The Unspoken Pain of Abortion* (Springfield, IL: Acorn, 2002), 189, 293; D. C. Reardon and P. G. Ney, "Abortion and Subsequent Substance Abuse," *American Journal of Drug and Alcohol Abuse* 26, no. 1 (2000): 61–75.

17. "Most Studies Show Abortion Linked to Increased Mental Health Problems," Elliot Institute, http://afterabortion.org/2011/most-studies-show-abortion-linked-to-increased-mental-health-problems.

18. Priscilla K. Coleman et al., "Associations between Voluntary and Involuntary Forms of Perinatal Loss and Child Maltreatment among Low-Income Mothers," *Acta Paediatrica* 94, no 10 (2005): 1476–1483.

19. Benedict et al., "Maternal Perinatal Risk Factors and Child Abuse," *Child Abuse and Neglect* 9 (1985): 217–224; P. G. Ney, "Relationship between Abortion and Child Abuse," *Canadian Journal of Psychiatry* 24 (1979): 610–620.

20. Catherine T. Coyle, "An Online Pilot Study to Investigate the Effects of Abortion on Men," Association

for Interdisciplinary Research in Values and Social Change, Research Bulletin 19, no. 1 (Winter 2006). http://www.abortion research.us/images/Vol19No1.pdf.

21. "Abortion for Profit," Abort73.com, http://www.abort 73.com/abortion/abortion_for_profit.

22. Mitch Behna, "The Economic Effect of Abortion: Billions and Billions Lost," LifeNews.com, July 16, 2012, http://www.lifenews.com/2012/07/16/the-economic-effect -of-abortion-billions-and-billions-lost.

23. Keith Riler, "Thirty-Six Couples Wait for Every One Baby Who is Adopted," LifeNews.com, July 9, 2012, http://www.lifenews.com/2012/07/09/thirty-six-couples -wait-for-every-one-baby-who-is-adopted.

24. Karen Pazol et al., *Morbidity and Mortality Weekly Report*, Abortion Surveillance—United States, 2007; Surveillance Summaries, February 25, 2011/60(SS01); 1–39, Division of Reproductive Health; National Center for Chronic Disease Prevention and Health Promotion, Centers for Disease Control and Prevention, http://www.cdc.gov/mmwr/preview/ mmwrhtml/ss6001a1.htm#Tab14.

25. "Planned Parenthood," BlackGenocide.org, http:// www.blackgenocide.org/planned.html.

26. Steve Mosher, "Twelve Out of Twelve Recent Studies Show Abortion Linked to Breast Cancer," LifeNews.com, http://www.lifenews.com/2014/09/22/twelve-out-of-twelve-recent-studies-show-abortion-linked-to-breast-cancer.

27. K. Schulz et al., "Measures to Prevent Cervical Injuries During Suction Curettage Abortion," *The Lancet* (May 28, 1983): 1182–1184; W. Cates, "The Risks Associated with Teenage Abortion," *New England Journal of Medicine*, 309(11): 612–624; R. Castadot, "Pregnancy Termination: Techniques, Risks, and Complications and Their Management," *Fertility and Sterility*, 45(1): 5–16.

28. Jeffrey M. Barrett, Frank H. Boehm, and Allen P. Killam, "Induced Abortion: A Risk Factor for Placenta Previa," *American Journal of Obstetrics and Gynecology* 171, issue 7 (December 1, 1981): 769–772.

29. J. G. Schenker and E. J. Margalioth. "Intrauterine Adhesions: An Updated Appraisal," *Fertility and Sterility* 37 (May 1982): 593–610.

30. Gissler, Hemminki, and Lonnqvist, "Suicides After Pregnancy in Finland."

31. Nathanson and Ostling, *Aborting America*, 254.

Chapter 18

1. Nathanson, *Hand of God*, 260.
2. Ibid., 198.
3. Ibid., 200.
4. Lorene Hanley Duquin, *A Century of Catholic Converts* (Huntington, IN: Our Sunday Visitor, 2003), 221.

Chapter 23

1. W. H. Lewis, ed., *Letters of C. S. Lewis* (New York: Mariner Books, 2003), 408.
2. "Life Will Triumph—Part 1" HM Television, https://www.youtube.com/watch?v=qThLwulQ8_o.

Chapter 24

1. John 8:12.
2. "Moloch/Molech," http://www.whale.to/b/moloch_s.htm.
3. Henry H. Halley, "Joshua, Chapters 23, 24," *Halley's Bible Handbook* (Grand Rapids, MI: Zondervan, 1962), 160.
4. "Nicki Minaj Opens Up About Abortion: It's 'Haunted Me All My Life,'" Yahoo TV, https://www.yahoo.com/tv/s/nicki-minaj-opens-abortion-haunted-224200037.html?nf=1.

5. "Inside Pregnancy: Your Baby's DNA," BabyCenter, http://www.babycenter.com/2_inside-pregnancy-your-babys-dna_10354440.bc.

6. Jodi Jacobson, "Life Begins At Conception. That's Not the Point," RH Reality Check, http://rhrealitycheck.org/article/2012/11/04/life-begins-at-conception-thats-not-point-0.